The Diatessaron of Tatian

The Diatessaron of Tatian

The Diatessaron of Tatian

© Lighthouse Publishing 2025

Written by: Tatian (120-180 AD)
Translated by: Rev. Hope W. Hogg (1863-1912)
Updated into Modern U.S English: A.M. Overett (b.1960)

All rights reserved. Without limiting the rights under copyright reserved above, no part of this publication may be reproduced, stored in a retrieval system, or transmitted, in any form or by any means (electronic, mechanical, photocopying, recording or otherwise), without the prior written permission of the copyright owner of this book.

Published by
Lighthouse Publishing
SAN 257-4330
228 Freedom Parkway
Hoschton, GA 30548
United States of America

www.lighthousechristianpublishing.com

Introduction.
───────────

The aim of the following introductory paragraphs is neither to furnish a detailed restatement of facts already known, nor to offer an independent contribution to the discussion of the problems that arise, although in other circumstances such an attempt might be made with advantage. All that is needed and practicable here is to describe briefly, if possible, the nature of the connection between the English treatise forming the next part of this volume and the ancient work known as the *Diatessaron* of Tatian; and then to indicate in a few words some of the more important or interesting features of the work itself, and some of the historical and other problems that are in one way or another connected with it.

1 *The Text Translated.*—What is offered to the reader is a translation into English of an Arabic text, published at Rome in 1888, in a volume entitled in Arabic *Diatessaron, which Titianus Compiled from the Four Gospels*, with the alternative Latin title, *Tatiani Evangeliorum Harmoniæ, Arabice*. The Roman volume consists of two parts—the text, covering a little over 209 very clearly printed Arabic pages, and a Latin half, comprising a scholarly introduction (pp. v.–xv.), a Latin translation (pp. 1–99), and a table showing the order in which the passages taken from the gospels occur in the text. The editor is P. Agostino Ciasca, a well-known Orientalist, "scriptor" at the Vatican Library.

2 *Former Translations.*—In his Introduction (p. xiv. f.) Ciasca explains that in his translation he aimed at preserving *quantum, salva fidelitate, integrum fuit, indolem stylumque Clementinæ Vulgate*. This Latin version was in its turn translated into English by the Rev.

J. Hamlyn Hill, B.D., and published in 1894 in a volume entitled *The Earliest Life of Christ*, with an interesting introduction and a number of valuable appendices. The ms. of Mr. Hill's translation of the Latin of Ciasca was compared with the Arabic original by Mr. G. Buchanan Gray, M.A., lecturer in Hebrew and the Old Testament in Mansfield College, Oxford.

3 *The Present Translation*.—the translation offered here is quite independent of either of these two. Ciasca's Latin was seldom consulted, except when it was thought the Arabic might perhaps be obscured by a misprint. After the translation was completed, Hill's English was compared with it to transfer Mr. Hill's valuable system of references to the margin of this work, and to lessen the risk of oversights passing the last revision unnoticed. In two or three cases this process led to the adoption of a different construction, and in a few of the more awkward passages a word was borrowed as being less harsh than that which had originally been written. Speaking generally, the present version appears to differ from Mr. Hill's in adhering more closely to the original.

4 *The Arabic Text*.—only two Arabic mss. are known to exist. Ciasca tells us (p. xiv.) that he took as the basis of his text that ms. which is more careful in its orthography, the Cod. Vat. Arab. No. 14. He, however, printed at the foot of the page the variants of the other ms., and supplied from it two lacunæ in the Cod. Vat., substituted its readings for those of the Cod. Vat. where he thought them preferable, and followed its testimony in omitting two important passages. Here and there Ciasca has emended the text, but he does not profess to have produced a critical edition.

5 *The Arabic mss.*—unfortunately, the present writer has not had an opportunity of examining these two mss.; but they have been described at some length by Ciasca; Codex XIV. in Pitra's *Analecta Sacra*, iv., 465 ff., and the other codex in the volume with which we are dealing, p. vi. ff. I. The former, which we shall call the Vatican ms. (in Ciasca's footnotes it is called A), was brought to the Vatican from the East by Joseph S. Assemani about a.d. 1719. It was described by Stephen E. Assemani, Rosenmüller, and Akerblad, and then at length by Ciasca, to whose account the reader must be referred for the details. It consists of 123 folios, of which the first seven are somewhat spoiled, and of which two are missing, and is supposed by Ciasca, from the character of the writing, and from the presence of certain Coptic letters by the first hand, to have been written in Egypt. S. Assemani assigned it to the twelfth century, and Ciasca accepts his verdict, while Akerblad says the thirteenth or fourteenth century. The text of the ms. is pretty fully vocalized, but there are few diacritical points. There are marginal notes, some of them by a later hand, which Ciasca classifies as (1) emendations, (2) restorations, (3) explanations. II. The second ms., which we shall call the Borgian (in Ciasca's footnotes it is called B), was brought to the Borgian Museum from Egypt in August, 1886. It has at the end the following inscription in Arabic: "A present from Halim Dos Ghali, the Copt, the Catholic, to the Apostolic See, in the year of Christ 1886." Antonius Morcos, Visitor Apostolic of the Catholic Copts, when, in the beginning of 1886, he was shown and informed about the Vatican ms., told of this other one and was the means of its being sent to Rome. The Borgian ms., which Ciasca refers to the fourteenth century, consists of 355 folios.

Folios 1–852*8* contain an anonymous preface on the gospels, briefly described by Ciasca, who, however, does not say whether it appears to have been originally written in Arabic or to have been translated into that language. With folios 96*b*, 97*a*, which are reproduced in phototype in Ciasca's edition, begins the Introductory Note given in full at the beginning of the present translation. The text of the *Diatessaron* ends on folio 353*a*, but is followed by certain appendices, for which see below, §55, 17, note. This ms. is complete, and has, as we shall see, in some respects a better text, though it is worse in its orthography than the Vatican ms.

6 *Condition of the Arabic Text*.—Ciasca's text does not profess to be critically determined, for which purpose a more careful study of each of the mss. and an estimate of their respective texts would be indispensable. Although the Borgian ms. is supposed by Ciasca to be a century or two later than the Vatican ms. it is clearly not a copy of the latter, for not only does it sometimes offer more original readings, but, as we shall see, its text in some points coincides more exactly in scope with the original work. The list of various readings supplied by Ciasca, which is equal to about a fifth or a quarter of the text itself, ought to yield, on being analyzed, some canons of criticism. The footnotes of the present edition are enough to show that a number of the peculiar features of Ciasca's text do not belong to the original Arabic ms.; and further study would dispose of still more. On the other hand, there are unfortunately some indications that the common ancestor of both mss., though perhaps less than two centuries removed from the original, was not the original itself, and therefore emendation may be necessary even where both mss. agree. From first to last it has to be

borne in mind that a great deal of work was done at Arabic versions of the gospels, and the text of the copy from which our two mss. are descended may already have suffered from contact with other versions; while the special activity of the thirteenth century may have left its mark in some places on the text of the Borgian ms., supposing it to be chronologically the later.

7 *Origin of the Arabic Text.*—if some of the uncouthness of the Arabic text is due to corruption in the course of transmission, much is also due to its being not an original work, but a translation. That it is, in the main, a translation from Syriac is too obvious to need proof. The Introductory Notice and Subscription to the Borgian ms., moreover, expressly state that the work was translated by one Abu'l Faraj 'Abdulla ibn-at-Tayyib, an "excellent and learned priest," and the inferiority of parts of the translation, and entire absence of any confirmatory evidence, hardly suffice to refute this assertion. Still, the Borgian ms. is a late witness, and although it most probably preserves a genuine tradition as to the author of our work, its statement need not therefore necessarily be correct in every point.

8 *The Arabic Editor and his Method.*—Ibn-at-Tayyib (d. 1043) is a well-known man, a Nestorian monk and scholar, secretary to Elias I., Patriarch of Nisibis (for references to sources see, e.g., Ciasca's Introduction, p. xi. f. and Steinschneider's long note in his *Polemische und apologetische Lit. in Arabische Sprache*, pp. 52–55). As we are here concerned with him simply as a link in the chain connecting our present work with its original source, the only point of interest for us is the method he followed in producing it. Did he prepare an independent translation or did he make use of existing Arabic versions,

his own or others'? Until this question which space forbids us to discuss here, has been more thoroughly investigated, it must suffice to say that in view of the features in the present text that have not yet been shown to exist in any other Arabic version, it is still at least a tenable hypothesis that Ibn-at-Tayyib's ms. constituted to a considerable extent a real translation rather than a sort of Arabic parallel to the Codex Fuldensis (see below, 12).

9 *The Syriac Text Translated*—The eleventh century ms. of Ibn-at-Tayyib, could we reach it, would bring us face to face with the more interesting question of the nature of his Syriac original. The Subscription to the Borgian ms. states, probably copying the statement from its exemplar, that this was a. Syriac ms. in the handwriting of 'Isa ibn-'Ali al Motatabbib, pupil of Honain ibn Ishak. This Honain was a famous Arabic physician and medical writer of Bagdad (d. 873), whose school produced quite a number of translations and translators, among whom Ibn-'Ali, supposed to be identical with the Syriac lexicographer of the same name, is known to have had a high place. The Syriac ms., therefore, that Ibnat- Tayyib translated takes us back to about the year 900. But the Subscription to each of our mss. states that the work ended is the gospel called *Diatessaron*, compiled from the four gospels by Titianus; while the Introductory Note to the Borgian ms. adds that this Titianus was a Greek. The next step, therefore, is to inquire whether any traces exist of such a Syriac work, or any statements by which we can check the account just given of it.

10 *Other Traces of a Syriac Text.*—No copy of a Syriac *Diatessaron* has yet been shown to have survived. A number of quotations40 from such a work have,

however, been found in a Syriac commentary on the New Testament by Isho'dad of Merv (*circ.* 852), a contemporary of Honain, Ibn-'Ali's teacher. The value of these extracts is apparent, for they take us back one generation earlier than Ibn-at-Tayyib's Syriac exemplar. More important still, they do not entirely agree with the text of our Arabic version. To solve the problem thus raised, we must examine some of the statements about the *Diatessaron* to be found in ecclesiastical writers.

11 *Statements about the Diatessaron.*—One of the most widely known is that of Isho'dad himself, who, in his Preface to the Gospel of Mark, says: "Tatian, disciple of Justin, the philosopher and martyr, selected from the four gospels, and combined and composed a gospel, and called it *Diatessaron*, i.e., the Combined,...and upon this gospel Mar Ephraem commented." Dionysius Bar Salibi (twelfth century) repeats each of these phrases, adding, "Its commencement was, 'In the beginning was the Word.'" These statements identify the author of the *Diatessaron* with a man otherwise known, and tell us that the great Syrian father Ephraem (d. 373) wrote a commentary on it. Unfortunately, no Syriac ms. of Ephraem's work is known to have survived; but quotations from it, or allusions to it, are being found in other Syriac writers. One further reference will suffice for the present. Theodoret, Bishop of Cyrrhus, four hundred years before Isho'dad, wrote thus in his book on Heresies (written in 453): "Tatian the Syrian....This [writer] also composed the gospel which is called *Diatessaron*, cutting out the genealogies and whatever other passages show that the Lord was born of the seed of David according to the flesh." Before examining the testimonials we have

now adduced, we must notice certain more remote sources of information.

12 *Non-Syriac Texts of the Diatessaron.*—Although Ephraem's Syriac commentary on the *Diatessaron* is for the present lost, there is an Armenian version of it extant in two mss. dating from about the time of Bar Salibi and our Vat. ms. A Latin translation of this work, published in 1876 by Moesinger, formed the main basis of Zahn's attempt to reconstruct the *Diatessaron*. Appendix X in Hill's *Diatessaron* (pp. 334–377) contains an English translation of the texts commented on by Ephraem, made from Moesinger's Latin, but collated with the Armenian by Professor J. Armitage Robinson, of Cambridge. A comparison of this document with our Arabic text shows a remarkable agreement in the order and contents, but just as remarkable a lack of agreement in the kind of text presented. The same phenomenon is met with when we compare our Arabic text with a document that carries us back three hundred years before the time of Isho'dad, and therefore more than six hundred years before the Armenian mss.—the Codex Fuldensis of the Vulgate. This ms. contains an arrangement of the gospel matter that its discoverer and publisher, Bishop Victor of Capua (d. 554), rightly concluded must represent the *Diatessaron* of Tatian, but for the text of which was apparently substituted that of the Vulgate. We are now ready to weigh the testimony we have gathered.

13 *Accretions to the Diatessaron.*—The statements we are to consider are: (1) Bar Salibi's, that Tatian's *Diatessaron* began with "In the beginning was the Word"; (2) Theodoret's, that Tatian cut out the genealogies; and (3) the same writer's, that Tatian also cut out "whatever other passages show that the Lord was born

of the seed of David according to the flesh." Of these statements 1 conflicts with the Arabic text, which begins with Mark, and the Codex Fuldensis, which begins with Luke, but agrees with the Ephraem source; the same is true of 2; while 3 conflicts with all three texts. Our limits do not admit of our discussing these points in detail. It must suffice to say (1) that, although a more careful examination at firsthand of the introductory notices in the two Arabic mss. seems needed before one can venture to propound a complete theory, a comparison of the two texts, and a consideration of the descriptions given by Ciasca and Lagarde, make it almost certain that the genuine Arabic text of Ibn-at-Tayyib began with John i. 1. Similarly the first four verses of Luke (on which see also below, § 1. 6, note) were probably not in the original text of the ms. that Victor found, for they are not mentioned in the (old) table of contents. We seem thus to detect a process of gradual accretion of material drawn from the ordinary gospel text. (2) The genealogies illustrate the same process. In the Vatican ms. they form part of the text. But in the Borgian ms., although they precede the Subscription, and therefore *may* have been already in the ninth century Syriac ms. used by Ibn-at-Tayyib, they are still placed by themselves, after a blank space, at the end of the volume, with a title of their own. Here, therefore, we actually see stages of the process of accretion. (3) It is therefore possible that the same account must also be given of 3, although in this case we have no direct proof.

14 *Passages Lost from the Diatessaron.*—If the Diatessaron has thus been growing so as to represent the ordinary text of the canonical gospels more completely, we have also evidence that suggests that it has been at some time or times purged of certain features that are

lacking in these canonical gospels. For one case of this kind see below, §4, 36, note.

15 *Presentation of the Text of the Diatessaron*.— we have observed already that the Latin, Armenian, and Arabic *Diatessarons* correspond pretty closely in subject matter and arrangement, but differ markedly in text. The Codex Fuldensis is really a ms. of the Vulgate, although the text that Victor found was probably somewhat different. The Armenian text differs materially from the ordinary Syriac version of the New Testament (the Peshitta), showing a marked connection with another type of Syriac text represented now by the Curetonian and Sinaitic (Lewis) mss. The Arabic text, on the other hand, almost systematically represents the Peshitta. The explanation of the condition of text in the Codex Fuldensis is obvious. On the other hand, the relationship of the Armenian and Arabic texts to the original *Diatessaron* must be determined by weighing very multifarious evidence that cannot be even cited here (see above 6 ff.). The two texts depend, as we have seen, on late mss. but all the earlier references and quotations go to show that the Armenian text stands much more closely related to the original than does the Arabic.

16 *Checkered History of the Diatessaron*.—What use the Arabic edition of Ibn-at-Tayyib was put to when made we do not know. 'Abd Isho' (d. 1318) speaks in the highest terms of Tatian's work, saying, "…With all diligence he attended to the utmost degree to the right order of those things which were said and done by the Savior; of his own he did not add a single saying." But the leaders of the Syrian church had not always thought so.

Theodoret (*loc. cit.*) some nine hundred years earlier had written thus: "...Even those that follow the apostolic doctrines, not perceiving the mischief of the composition," used "the book too simply as an abridgment." A few years earlier Rabbula, Bishop of Edessa (d. 435), had said: "Let the presbyters and deacons give heed that in all the churches there be provided and read a copy of the Distinct Gospel," i.e., not the harmonized or mixed gospel. But obviously these men were trying to suppress traditional practice due to very different views. Theodoret (*loc. cit.*) found more than two hundred copies of the work "held in respect in the churches"; and the *Doctrine of Addai* (Edessa, third to fourth century) seems simply to identify the *Diatessaron* and the New Testament. Outside of the Syriac speaking churches we find no signs of any such use of the *Diatessaron*. It would seem, therefore, that at a quite early stage the *Diatessaron* was very widely if not universally read in the Syriac churches, and commented on by scholars as the gospel; that in time it fell under the condemnation of some at least of the church leaders, who made violent efforts to suppress it; that it could not be suppressed; that a commentary on it was (perhaps in the fifth century) translated into Armenian; that it was still discussed by commentators, and new Syriac mss. of it made in the ninth century, and thought worth the labor of reproduction in Arabic in the beginning of the eleventh century; that mss. of the Armenian volume continued to be made down to the very end of the twelfth century, and of the Arabic edition down to the fourteenth century; but that this long life was secured at the expense of a more or less rapid assimilation of the text to that of the great

Syriac Bible which from the fourth century onwards became more and more exclusively used—the Peshitta.

17 *The Author of the Diatessaron.*—The *Diatessaron* is such an impersonal work that we do not need to know very much about its compiler. It will suffice here to say that he tells us himself that he was born "in the land of the Assyrians," and brought up a heathen. After travelling in search of knowledge, he settled at Rome, where he became a pupil of Justin Martyr, professed Christianity, and wrote in Greek his *Address to the Greeks*, translated in vol. iii. of the *Ante-Nicene Christian Library*. He was too independent in his attitude to maintain a permanent popularity, and after Justin's death left Rome and returned to Mesopotamia. It was probably here that he issued in Syriac his most important work, the *Diatessaron*, which won such a warm place in the heart of the Syrian church. Among the Greek scholars, however, he became more and more regarded as a heretic, Encratite (ascetic), and Gnostic.

18 *The Diatessaron as a Harmony.*—Not very much need be said on this subject, as every reader can collect the facts for himself. In its present form the Harmony draws from all the four canonical gospels, and from very little else. Opinions differ as to whether it originally indicated the gospel from which any given piece was drawn, and some uncertainty must remain in special cases as to what gospel actually has been drawn upon. Professor G. F. Moore, in a very interesting article on the *Diatessaron*, having counted the references in the Arabic mss., states that the Arabic text contains 50 percent of Mark, 66 percent of Luke, 76.5 percent of Matthew, and 96 percent of John. The summation of his figures gives the following result: out of a total of 3780

verses in the four gospels, the *Diatessaron* quotes 2769 and omits 1011. As to the order in which the whole is arranged, Moore thinks that Matthew has chiefly been followed; while Zahn regards the Fourth Gospel as normative. For a specimen of the way in which words and phrases from the different gospels are woven together, we may refer to § 52, 35 ff., and the notes thereon. In the Arabic mss., and probably in the Syriac exemplar, the work is divided into fifty-four almost equal chapters, followed by one short one—a feature that agrees well with what we have learned of the work as being of old the lectionary of the Syrian church.

19 *Problems Connected with the Diatessaron.*— The *Diatessaron* opens up a very wide field of study. A few points may be here enumerated (see also above, 8, and note there). In what language was it written? On the view favored by an increasing majority of scholars, that it was written in Syriac, was it a translation or simply a compilation? What precisely is its relation to the Syriac versions and the "Western" text generally? Then there is its bearing on the date and formation of the canonical gospels; the phenomenon of its so long supplying the place of those gospels; the analogy it presents to the Pentateuch, according to the critical view of the origin of the latter. These and other issues make the *Diatessaron* an important and interesting study.

20 *The Present Translation.*—the work of translation has been found much more tedious than was anticipated, notwithstanding the fact that considerably more than half of it is the work of my wife, which I have simply revised with special attention to the many obscurities dealt with in the footnotes. We have, however, worked so much together that it is very doubtful whether

anyone could assign the various parts to their respective sources. My wife also verified the Arabic references to the gospels printed on the margin to the right of the text, and prepared the Index to these references—an extremely laborious and perplexing piece of work. This Index is inserted merely for the practical purpose of enabling the reader to find any given gospel piece in the Diatessaron. When a verse is not found in the Index, an equivalent passage from some of the other gospels should be looked for. On the margin to the left of the text are indicated the pages of the Arabic text and the sections and verses in Hill's version.

The aim has been to make a literal translation. As two freer translations already exist, it seemed best to incline to the side of being over literal. If, however, features due simply to *Arabic* idiom have been preserved, this is an oversight. Uniformity could only have been secured by devoting a much longer time to the work than the editor was able to allow. The difficulties are due to the corrupt state of the Arabic text, and to the awkward reproduction or actual misunderstanding of the Syriac original by the author or authors of the Arabic translation. It has been impossible to maintain consistency in dealing with these phenomena. If any rendering seem strange, it will be well to consult the Syriac versions before deciding that it is wrong. A good deal of attention, too, has to be paid to the usage of the Arabic text, which, though it has many points of contact with other Arabic versions of the gospels, e.g., the ms. described by Gildemeister (*De evangg. in arab. e simp. Syr.*, 1865), is as yet for us (see above, 8) a distinct version, possessed of an individuality of its own, one pronounced feature being its very close adherence to its Syriac original. Another revision of the present translation, in the light of a fuller study of these features, would doubtless lead to changes both in the text and in the footnotes. The latter aim at preventing misunderstanding and giving some examples of the peculiarities of the text, and of the differences between the mss. To have dealt systematically with the text and various readings would have required much more time and space than was available. The consequence of this incompleteness has been some uncertainty at times what text to translate. As already stated (paragraphs 4 and 6), Ciasca's printed text neither represents any one ms. nor professes to be based in its eclecticism on any systematic critical principles. On the whole Ciasca has here been followed somewhat mechanically in deciding what to exhibit in the text and what to relegate to the footnotes. As a rule conjectural emendations have not been admitted into the *text* except where the ms. readings would hardly bear translation. Italics in the text denote words supplied for the sake of English idiom; in the footnotes, quotations from the mss. It is to be noted that many linguistic usages said, for shortness, in the footnotes to be characteristic of the present work, i.e., as compared with ordinary Arabic, are common in Arabic versions. "Syriac versions" means the three (Pesh., Cur., Sin.), or as many of them as contain the passage in question; if the Peshitta alone is quoted, it may be assumed that Cur. and Sin. are missing or diverge.

In conclusion we may say that an effort has been made to preserve even the order of words; but it must be emphasized that it is very doubtful whether it is wise for anyone to use the Arabic *Diatessaron* for critical purposes who is not acquainted with Arabic and Syriac. The tenses, e.g., are much vaguer in Arabic than in Greek and English, and are, moreover, in this work often accommodated to Syriac idiom. The Greek and the Revised Version have been used to determine in almost every case how the vague Arabic tenses and conjunctions should be rendered. It is therefore only where it *differs* from these that our translation can be quoted without investigation as giving positive evidence.

This is not a final translation. Few books have had a more remarkable literary history than the *Diatessaron*, and that history is by no means done. Much careful argument will yet be devoted to it, and perhaps discoveries as important as any hitherto made are yet to shed light on the problems that encircle it. If our work can help anyone to take a step in advance, we shall not regret the toil.

Oxford, 21st December, 1895.

Introductory Notes.

1. In the Borgian Ms.

In the name of the one God, the Father, and the Son, and the Holy Spirit, to him be the glory forever. We shall begin, with the help of God most high, the writing of the pure gospel, the blooming garden, called *Diatessaron* (a word meaning "fourfold"), the work compiled by Titianus the Greek out of the four evangelists—Matthew the elect, whose symbol is M, Mark the chosen, whose symbol is R, Luke the approved, whose symbol is K, and John the beloved, whose symbol is H. The work was translated from Syriac into Arabic by the excellent and learned priest Abu'l Faraj 'Abdulla ibn-at-Tayyib, may God grant him his favor. He began with the first of and he said: The Beginning of the Gospel of Jesus the Son of the living God. John: In the beginning, etc.

2. In the Vatican ms.

In the name of the Father, and the Son, and the Holy Spirit, giver of life, the God that is one in substance in his essence, and three in persons in his attributes. The first of his Gospel is He began the first of his Gospel with Mark. And he said: The Beginning of the Gospel of Jesus the Son of the living God. John: In the beginning, etc.

The Text of the Diatessaron.

[Section I]

[1] In the beginning was the Word, and the Word was with God, and God is the [2,3] Word. This *was* in the beginning with God. Everything was by his hand, and [4] without him not even one existing thing was *made*. In him was life, and the life [5] is the light of men. And the light shined in the darkness, and the darkness apprehended it not. [6] There was in the days of Herod the king a priest whose name was Zacharias, of the family of Abijah; and his wife was of the daughters of Aaron, and her name [7] was Elizabeth. And they were both righteous before God, walking in all his commands, [8] and in the uprightness of God without reproach. And they had no son, for [9] Elizabeth was barren, and they had both advanced in age. And while he discharged [10] [Arabic, p. 2] the duties of priest in the order of his service before God, according to the custom of the priesthood it was his turn to burn incense; so he entered the [11] temple of the Lord. And the whole gathering of the people were praying without at the [12] time of the incense. And there appeared unto Zacharias the angel of the Lord, standing [13] at the right of the altar of incense; and Zacharias was troubled when he saw him, [14] and fear fell upon him. But the angel

said unto him, Be not agitated, Zacharias, for thy prayer is heard, and thy wife Elizabeth shall bear thee a son, and thou shalt [15] call his name John; and thou shalt have joy and gladness, and many shall rejoice [16] at his birth. And he shall be great before the Lord, and shall not drink wine nor strong drink, and he shall be filled with the Holy Spirit while he is in his mother's [17] womb. And he shall turn back many of the children of Israel to the Lord their [18] God. And he shall go before him in the spirit, and in the power of Elijah the prophet, to turn back the heart of the fathers to the sons, and those that obey not to the knowledge of the righteous; and to prepare for the Lord a perfect people. [19] And Zacharias said unto the angel, How shall I know this, since I am an old man [20] and my wife is advanced in years? And the angel answered and said unto him, I am Gabriel, that stands before God; and I was sent to speak unto thee, and give [21] thee tidings of this. Henceforth thou shalt be speechless, and shalt not be able to speak until the day in which this shall come to pass, because thou didst not trust [22] this my word, which shall be accomplished in its time. 1And the people were standing [Arabic, p. 3] awaiting Zacharias, and they were perplexed at his delaying in the temple. [23] And when Zacharias went out, he was not able to speak unto them: so they knew that he had seen in the temple a vision; and he made signs unto them, and [24] continued dumb. And when the days of his service were completed, he departed to his dwelling. [25] And after those days Elizabeth his wife conceived; and she hid herself five [26] months, and said, This hath the Lord done unto me in the days when he looked upon me, to remove my reproach from among men. [27] And in the sixth month Gabriel the angel was sent from God to Galilee to a [28] city called

Nazareth, 108to a virgin given in marriage to a man named Joseph, of the [29] house of David; and the virgin's name was Mary. And the angel entered unto her and said unto her, Peace be unto thee, thou who art filled with grace. Our Lord [30] is with thee, thou blessed amongst women. And she, when she beheld, was agitated [31] at his word, and pondered what this salutation could be. And the angel said unto [32] her, Fear not, Mary, for thou hast found favor with God. Thou shalt now conceive, [33] and bear a son, and call his name Jesus. This shall be great, and shall be called the Son of the Most High; and the Lord God will give him the throne of [34] David his father: and he shall rule over the house of Jacob forever; and to his [35] kingdom there shall be no end. Mary said unto the angel, How shall this be to [36] me when no man hath known me? The angel answered and said unto her, The [Arabic, p. 4] Holy Spirit will come, and the power of the Most High shall rest upon thee, and therefore shall *he* that is born of thee be pure, and shall be called the Son [37] of God. And lo, Elizabeth thy kinswoman, she also hath conceived a son in her old [38] age; and this is the sixth month with her, her that is called barren. 118For nothing is [39] difficult for God. Mary said, Lo, I am the handmaid of the Lord; let it be unto me according unto thy word. And the angel departed from her.

[40] And then Mary arose in those days and went in haste into the hill country, to a [41] city of Judah; and entered into the house of Zacharias, and asked for the health of [42] Elizabeth. And when Elizabeth heard the salutation of Mary, the babe leaped in [43] her womb. And Elizabeth was filled with the Holy Spirit; and cried with a loud voice and said unto Mary, Blessed art thou amongst women, and blessed is the [44] fruit that is in thy

womb. Whence have I this *privilege*, that the mother of my [45] Lord should come unto me? When the sound of thy salutation reached my ears, [46] with great joy rejoiced the babe in my womb. And blessed is she who believed [47] that what was spoken *to her* from the Lord would be fulfilled. And Mary said,

My soul doth magnify the Lord,

[48] And my spirit hath rejoiced in God my Savior,

[49] Who hath looked upon the low estate of his handmaiden: Lo, henceforth, all generations shall pronounce blessing on me.

[50] For he hath done great things for me, who is mighty, And holy is his name.

[51] And his mercy embraces them who fear him, Throughout the ages and the times.

[52] [Arabic, p. 5] He wrought the victory with his arm, and scattered them that prided themselves in their opinions.

[53] He overthrew them that acted haughtily from their thrones, and raised the lowly.

[54] He satisfied with good things the hungry, and left the rich without anything.

[55] He helped Israel his servant, and remembered his mercy

[56] (According as he spoke with our fathers) Unto Abraham and unto his seed forever.

[57] And Mary abode with Elizabeth about three months, and returned unto her house.

[58, 59] And Elizabeth's time of delivery was come; and she brought forth a son. And her neighbors and kinsfolk heard that God had multiplied his mercy towards her; [60] and they rejoiced with her. And when it was the

eighth day, they came to circumcise the child, and called him Zacharias, *calling him* by the name of his father. [61] And his mother answered and said unto them, Not so; but he shall be called John. [62] And they said unto her, There is no man of thy kindred that is called by this name. [63, 64] And they made signs to his father, *saying*, How dost thou wish to name him? And he asked for a tablet, and wrote and said, His name is John. And every one wondered. [65] And immediately his mouth was opened, and his tongue, and he spoke and [66] praised God. And fear fell on all their neighbors: and this was spoken of in all [67] the mountains of Judah. And all who heard pondered in their hearts and said, What shall this child be? And the hand of the Lord was with him.

[68] And Zacharias his father was filled with the Holy Spirit, and prophesied and said,

[69] Blessed is the Lord, the God of Israel,

Who hath cared for his people, and wrought for it salvation;

[70] And hath raised for us the horn of salvation [Arabic, p. 6] In the house of David his servant

[71] (As he spoke by the mouth of his holy prophets from eternity),

[72] That he might save us from our enemies,

And from the hand of all them that hate us.

[73] And he hath performed his mercy towards our fathers, And remembered his holy covenants,

[74] And the oath which he swore unto Abraham our father,

[75] That he would give us deliverance from the hand of our enemies, And without fear we shall serve before him

[76] All our days with equity and righteousness.

[77] And as for thee, O child, prophet of the Most High shalt thou be called. Thou shalt go forth before the face of the Lord to prepare his way,
[78] To give the knowledge of salvation unto his people, For the forgiveness of their sins,
[79] Through the mercy of the compassion of our God, With which he cares for us, to appear from on high
[80] To give light to them that sit in darkness and under the shadow of death, And to set straight our feet in the way of peace.
[81] And the child grew and became strong in the spirit, and abode in the desert until the time of his appearing unto the children of Israel.

Section II.
[1] [Arabic, p. 7] Now the birth of Jesus the Messiah was on this wise: In the time when his mother was given in marriage to Joseph, before they came together, [2] she was found with child of the Holy Spirit. And Joseph her husband was a just *man* and did not wish to expose her, and he purposed to put her away secretly. [3] But when he thought of this, the angel of the Lord appeared unto him in a dream, and said unto him, Joseph, son of David, fear not to take Mary thy wife, for that [4] which is begotten in her is of the Holy Spirit. She shall bear a son, and thou shalt [5] call his name Jesus, and he shall save his people from their sins. And all this was that the saying from the Lord by the prophet might be fulfilled:
[6] Behold, the virgin shall conceive, and bear a son, And they shall call his name Immanuel,
[7] which is, being interpreted, With us is our God. And when Joseph arose from his [8] sleep, he did as

the angel of the Lord commanded him, and took his wife; and knew her not until she brought forth her firstborn son.

[9] And in those days there went forth a decree from Augustus Cæsar that all the [10] people of his dominion should be enrolled. This first enrolment was while Quirinius [11, 12] was governor of Syria. And every man went to be enrolled in his city. And Joseph went up also from Nazareth, a city of Galilee, to Judæa, to the city of David [13] which is called Bethlehem (for he was of the house of David and of his tribe), with [14] [Arabic, p. 8] Mary his betrothed, she being with child, to be enrolled there. And while [15] she was there the days for her being delivered were accomplished. And she brought forth her firstborn son; and she wrapped him in swaddling clothes and laid him in a manger, because there was no place for them where they were staying.

[16] And there were in that region shepherds abiding, keeping their flock in the watch [17] of the night. And behold, the angel of God came unto them, and the glory of the [18] Lord shone upon them; and they were greatly terrified. And the angel said unto them, Be not terrified; for I bring you tidings of great joy which shall be to the [19] whole world; there is born to you this day a Savior, which is the Lord the Messiah, [20] in the city of David. And this is a sign for you: ye shall find a babe wrapped [21] in swaddling clothes and laid in a manger. And there appeared with the angels suddenly many heavenly forces praising God and saying,

[22] Praise be to God in the highest,
And on the earth peace, and good hope to men.

[23] And when the angels departed from them to heaven, the shepherds spoke to one another and said, We will go to Bethlehem and see this word which hath been,

as [24] the Lord made known unto us. And they came with haste, and found Mary and [25] Joseph, and the babe laid in a manger. And when they saw, they reported the word [26] which was spoken to them about the child. And all that heard wondered at the [27] description which the shepherds described to them. But Mary kept these sayings [28] and discriminated them in her heart. And those shepherds returned, magnifying and praising God for all that they had seen and heard, according as it was described unto them.

[29] [Arabic, p. 9] And when eight days were fulfilled that the child should be circumcised, his name was called Jesus, being that by which he was called by the angel before his conception in the womb.

[30] And when the days of their purification according to the law of Moses were [31] completed, they took him up to Jerusalem to present him before the Lord (as it is written in the law of the Lord, Every male opening the womb shall be called the [32] holy *thing* of the Lord), and to give a sacrificial victim as it is said in the law of [33] the Lord, A pair of doves or two young pigeons. And there was in Jerusalem a man whose name was Simeon; and this man was upright and pious, and expecting [34] the consolation of Israel; and the Holy Spirit was upon him. And it had been said unto him by the Holy Spirit, that he should not see death till he had seen with [35] his eyes the Messiah of the Lord.

And this man came by the Spirit to the temple; and at the time when his parents brought in the child Jesus, that they might [36] present for him a sacrifice, as it is written in the law, he bare him in his arms and praised God and said,

[37] Now loosest thou the bonds of thy servant, O Lord, in peace, According to thy saying;

[38] For mine eye hath witnessed thy mercy,

[39] Which thou hast made ready because of the whole world;

[40] A light for the unveiling of the nations, And a glory to thy people Israel.

[41] And Joseph and his mother were marveling at the things which were being said

[42] concerning him. And Simeon blessed them and said to Mary his mother, Behold, he is set for the overthrow and rising of many in Israel; and for a sign of contention; [43] and a spear shall pierce through thine own soul; that the thoughts of the [44] [Arabic, p. 10] hearts of many may be revealed. And Anna the prophetess, the daughter of Phanuel, of the tribe of Asher, was also advanced in years (and she dwelt [45] with her husband seven years from her virginity, and she remained a widow about eighty-four years); and she left not the temple, and served night and day with [46] fasting and prayer. And she also rose in that hour and thanked the Lord, and she [47] spoke of him with everyone who was expecting the deliverance of Jerusalem. And when they had accomplished everything according to what is in the law of the Lord, they returned to Galilee, to Nazareth their city.

Section III.

[1, 2] And after that, the Magi came from the east to Jerusalem, and said, Where is the King of the Jews which was born? We have seen his star in the east, and have [3] come to worship him. And Herod the king heard,

and he was troubled, and all [4] Jerusalem with him. And he gathered all the chief priests and the scribes of the [5] people, and asked them in what place the Messiah should be born. They said, In Bethlehem of Judæa: thus it is written in the prophet,

[6] Thou also, Bethlehem of Judah,
Art not contemptible among the kings of Judah:
From thee shall go forth a king,
And he shall be a shepherd to my people Israel.

[7] Then Herod called the Magi secretly, and inquired of them the time at which [8] the star appeared to them. And he sent them to Bethlehem, and said unto them, Go and search about the child diligently; and when ye have found him, come and [9] make known to me, that I also may go and worship him. And they, when they [Arabic, p. 11] heard the king, departed; and lo, the star which they had seen in the east went before them, until it came and stood above the place where the child [10, 11] was. And when they beheld the star, they rejoiced with very great joy. And they entered the house and beheld the child with Mary his mother, and fell down worshipping him, and opened their saddle-bags and offered to him offerings, gold and [12] myrrh and frankincense. And they saw in a dream that they should not return to Herod, and they travelled by another way in going to their country.

[13] And when they had departed, the angel of the Lord appeared in a dream to Joseph, and said unto him, Rise, take the child and his mother, and flee into Egypt, and be thou there until I speak to thee; for Herod is determined to seek the child [14] to slay him. And Joseph arose and took the child and his mother in the night, and

[15] fled into Egypt, and remained in it until the time of the death of Herod: that that might be fulfilled which was said by the Lord in the prophet, which said, From [16] Egypt did I call my son. And Herod then, when he saw that he was mocked of the Magi, was very angry, and sent and killed all the male children which were in Bethlehem and all its borders, from two years old and under, according to the time [17] which he had inquired from the Magi. Then was fulfilled the saying in Jeremiah the prophet, which said,

[18] A voice was heard in Ramah,
Weeping and much lamentation;
Rachel weeping for her children,
And not willing to be consoled for their loss.

[19] But when Herod the king died, the angel of the Lord appeared in a dream to [20] Joseph in Egypt, and said unto him, Rise and take the child and his mother, and [Arabic, p. 12] go into the land of Israel; for they have died who sought the child's life. [21] And Joseph rose and took the child and his mother, and came to the land [22] of Israel. But when he heard that Archelaus had become king over Judæa instead of Herod his father, he feared to go thither; and he saw in a dream that he should [23] go into the land of Galilee, and that he should abide in a city called Nazareth: that the saying in the prophet might be fulfilled, that he should be called a Nazarene.

[24] And the child grew, and became strong in spirit, becoming filled with wisdom; and the grace of God was upon him.

[25] And his kinsfolk used to go every year to Jerusalem at the feast of the Passover.

[26] And when he was twelve years old, they went up according to their custom, [27] to the feast. And when

the days were accomplished, they returned; and the child [28] Jesus remained in Jerusalem, and Joseph and his mother knew not: and they supposed that he was with the children of their company. And when they had gone one day's journey, they sought him beside their people and those who knew them, [29] and they found him not; so they returned to Jerusalem and sought him again. [30] And after three days they found him in the temple, sitting in the midst of the teachers, [31] hearing them and asking them *questions*; and all who heard him wondered at [32] his wisdom and his words. And when they saw him they wondered, and his mother said unto him, My son, why hast thou dealt with us thus? Behold, I and thy father [33] have been seeking for thee with much anxiety. And he said unto them, Why were [34] ye seeking me? Know ye not that I must be in the house of my Father? And they [35] understood not the word which he spoke unto them. And he went down with them, and came to Nazareth; and he was obedient to them: and his mother used to keep all these sayings in her heart.

[36] [Arabic, p. 13] And Jesus grew in his stature and wisdom, and in grace with God and men.

[37] And in the fifteenth year of the reign of Tiberius Cæsar, when Pontius Pilate was governor in Judæa, and one of the four rulers, Herod, in Galilee; and Philip his brother, one of the four rulers, in Ituræa and in the district of Trachonitis; and [38] Lysanias, one of the four rulers, in Abilene; in the chief-priesthood of Annas and Caiaphas, the command of God went forth to John the son of Zacharias in the [39] desert. And he came into all the region which is about Jordan, proclaiming the [40] baptism of repentance unto the forgiveness of sins. 281And he was preaching in the [41] wilderness of

Judæa, and saying, Repent ye; the kingdom of heaven is come near. [42] This is he that was spoken *of* in Isaiah the prophet,

> The voice which cries in the desert,
> [43] Prepare ye the way of the Lord,
> And make straight in the plain, paths for our God.
> [44] All the valleys shall become filled,
> And all the mountains and hills shall become low;
> And the rough shall become plain, And the difficult place, easy;
> [45] And all flesh shall see the salvation of God.

[46] This *man* came to bear witness, that he might bear witness to the light, that [47] every man might believe through his mediation. He was not the light, but that he [48] might bear witness to the light, which was the light of truth that giveth light to [49] every man coming into the world. He was in the world, and the world was made [50] by him, and the world knew [51] him not. He came unto his own, and his own received him not. And those who received him, to them gave he the power that they might [52] be sons of God,—those which believe in his name: which were born, not of blood, [53] nor of the will of the flesh, nor of the will of a man, but of God. And the Word became flesh, and took up his abode among us; and we saw his glory as the glory [54] of the only *Son* from the Father, which is full of grace and equity. John bare witness [Arabic, p. 14] of him, and cried, and said, This is he that I said cometh after me and [55] was before me, because he was before me. And of his fullness received [56] we all grace for grace. For the law was given through the mediation of Moses, but truth and grace were through Jesus Christ.

Section IV.

[1] No man hath seen God at any time; the only *Son*, God, which is in the bosom of his Father, he hath told of *him*.

[2] And this is the witness of John when the Jews sent to him from Jerusalem priests [3] and Levites to ask him, Who art thou? And he acknowledged, and denied not; [4] and he confessed that he was not the Messiah. And they asked him again, What then? Art thou Elijah? And he said, I am not he. Art thou a prophet? He [5] said, No. They said unto him, Then who art thou? that we may answer them that [6] sent us. What says thou of thyself? And he said, I am the voice that cries in [7] the desert, Repair ye the way of the Lord, as said Isaiah the prophet. And they [8] that were sent were from the Pharisees. And they asked him and said unto him, Why baptizes thou now, when thou art not the Messiah, nor Elijah, nor a prophet? [9] John answered and said unto them, I baptize with water: among you is standing [10] one whom ye know not: this is he who I said cometh after me and was before [11] me, the latchets of whose shoes I am not worthy to unloose. And that was in Bethany beyond Jordan, where John was baptizing.

[12] Now John's raiment was camel's hair, and *he was* girded with skins, and his food [13] [Arabic, p. 15] was of locusts and honey of the wilderness. Then went out unto him the people of Jerusalem, and all Judæa, and all the region which is about the [14, 15] Jordan; and they were baptized of him in the river Jordan, confessing their sins. But when he saw many of the Pharisees and Sadducees coming to be baptized, he said unto them, You children of vipers, who hath led you to flee from the wrath to come? [16, 17] Do now the fruits which are

worthy of repentance; and think and say not within yourselves, We have a father, *even* Abraham; for I say unto you, that God is able to [18] raise up of these stones children unto Abraham. Behold, the axe hath been laid at the roots of the trees, and so every tree that bears not good fruit shall be taken and [19] cast into the fire. And the multitudes were asking him and saying, What shall we do? [20] He answered and said unto them, He that hath two tunics shall give to him that [21] hath not; and he that hath food shall do likewise. And the publicans also came [22] to be baptized, and they said unto him, Teacher, what shall we do? He said unto [23] them, Seek not more than what ye are commanded to seek. And the servants of the guard asked him and said, And we also, what shall we do? He said unto them, Do not violence to any man, nor wrong him; and let your allowances satisfy you.

[24] And when the people were conjecturing about John, and all of them thinking [25] in their hearts whether he were haply the Messiah, John answered and said unto them, I baptize you with water; there cometh one after me who is stronger than I, the latchets of whose shoes I am not worthy to loosen; he will baptize you with the [26] Holy Spirit and fire: who taketh the fan in his hand to cleanse his threshing-floors, [Arabic, p. 16] and the wheat he gathered into his garners, while the straw he shall burn in fire which cannot be put out.

[27] And other things he taught and preached among the people.

[28] Then came Jesus from Galilee to the Jordan to John, to be baptized of him. [29] And Jesus was about thirty years old, and it was supposed that he was the son of [30] Joseph. And John saw Jesus coming unto him, and said, This is the Lamb of [31] God, that taketh on itself

the burden of the sins of the world! This is he concerning whom I said, There cometh after me a man who was before me, because he was [32] before me. And I knew him not; but that he should be made manifest to Israel, [33] for this cause came I to baptize with water. And John was hindering him and [34] saying, I have need of being baptized by thee, and comes thou to me? Jesus answered him and said, Suffer this now: thus it is our duty to fulfill all righteousness. [35] Then he suffered him. And when all the people were baptized, Jesus also [36] was baptized. And immediately he went up out of the water, and heaven opened [37] [Arabic, p. 17] to him, and the Holy Spirit descended upon him in the similitude of the [38] body of a dove; and lo, a voice from heaven, saying, This is my beloved [39] Son, in whom I am well pleased. And John bare witness and said, I beheld the [40] Spirit descend from heaven like a dove; and it abode upon him. But I knew him not; but he that sent me to baptize with water, he said unto me, Upon whomsoever thou shalt behold the Spirit descending and lighting upon him, the same is he that [41] baptizes with the Holy Spirit. And I have seen and borne witness that this is the Son of God.

[42, 43] And Jesus returned from the Jordan, filled with the Holy Spirit. And immediately the Spirit took him out into the wilderness, to be tried of the devil; and he [44] was with the beasts. And he fasted forty days and forty nights. And he ate nothing [45] in those days, and at the end of them he hungered. And the tempter came and said unto him, If thou art the Son of God, speak, and these stones shall become [46] bread. He answered and said, It is written, Not by bread alone shall man live, but [47] by every word that proceeded out of the mouth of God. Then the devil brought [48] him to the holy city, and set him on

the pinnacle of the temple, and said unto him, If thou art the Son of God, cast thyself down: for it is written,
He shall give his angels charge concerning thee:
And they shall take thee on their arms,
So that thy foot shall not stumble against a stone.
[49] Jesus said unto him, And it is written also, Thou shalt not tempt the Lord your [50] God. And the devil took him up to a high mountain, and shewed him all the kingdoms [51] [Arabic, p. 18] of the earth, and their glory, in the least time; and the devil said unto him, To thee will I give all this dominion, and its glory, which is delivered to [52] me that I may give it to whomsoever I will. If then thou wilt worship before me, all of it shall be thine.

Section V.
[1] Jesus answered and said unto him, Get thee hence, Satan: for it is written, Thou [2] shalt worship the Lord thy God, and him alone shalt thou serve. And when the [3] devil had completed all his temptations, he departed from him for a season. And behold, the angels drew near and ministered unto him.
[4, 5] And next day John was standing, and two of his disciples; and he saw Jesus as [6] he was walking, and said, Behold, the Lamb of God! And his two disciples heard [7] him saying *this*, and they followed Jesus. And Jesus turned and saw them coming after him, and said unto them, What seek you? They said unto him, Our master, [8] where art thou staying? And he said unto them, Come and see. And they came and saw his place, and abode with him that day: and it was about the tenth hour. [9] One of the two which heard from John, and followed Jesus, was Andrew the [10] brother of Simon.

And he saw first Simon his brother, and said unto him, We have [11] found the Messiah. And he brought him unto Jesus. And Jesus looked upon him and said, Thou art Simon, son of Jonah: thou shalt be called Cephas.

[12] And on the next day Jesus desired to go forth to Galilee, and he found Philip, [13] [Arabic, p. 19] and said unto him, Follow me. Now Philip was of Bethsaida, of the city [14] of Andrew and Simon. And Philip found Nathanael, and said unto him, He of whom Moses did write in the law and in the prophets, we have found that [15] he is Jesus the son of Joseph of Nazareth. Nathanael said unto him, Is it possible that there can be any good thing from Nazareth? Philip said unto him, Come and [16] see. And Jesus saw Nathanael coming to him, and said of him, This is indeed a [17] son of Israel in whom is no guile. And Nathanael said unto him, Whence knows thou me? Jesus said unto him, Before Philip called thee, while thou was under the [18] fig tree, I saw thee. Nathanael answered and said unto him, My Master, thou art [19] the Son of God; thou art the King of Israel. Jesus said unto him, Because I said unto thee, I saw thee under the fig tree, hast thou believed? Thou shalt see what is [20] greater than this. And he said unto him, Verily, verily, I say unto you, Henceforth ye shall see the heavens opened, and the angels of God ascending and descending upon the Son of man.

[21] And Jesus returned in the power of the Spirit to Galilee.

[22] And on the third day there was a feast in Cana, a city of Galilee; and the [23] mother of Jesus was there: and Jesus also and his disciples were invited to the [24] feast. And they lacked wine: and his mother said unto Jesus, They have no wine. [25] And Jesus said unto

her, What have I to do with thee, woman? hath not mine [26] hour come? And his mother said unto the servants, What he says unto you, do. [27] And there were there six vessels of stone, placed for the Jews' purification, such as [28] [Arabic, p. 20] would contain two or three jars. And Jesus said unto them, Fill the vessels

[29] with water. And they filled them to the top. He said unto them, Draw [30] out now, and present to the ruler of the feast. And they did *so*. And when the ruler of the company tasted that water which had become wine, and knew not whence it was (but the servants knew, because they filled up the water), the ruler of the company called [31] the bridegroom, and said unto him, Every man presented first the good wine, and on intoxication he brings what is poor; but thou hast kept the good wine until [32] now. And this is the first sign which Jesus did in Cana of Galilee, and manifested [33] his glory; and his disciples believed on him. And his fame spread in all the country [34] which was around them. And he taught in their synagogues, and was glorified [35] by every man. And he came to Nazareth, where he had been brought up, and entered, according to his custom, into the synagogue on the Sabbath day, and stood [36] up to read. And he was given the book of Isaiah the prophet. And Jesus opened the book and found the place where it was written,

[37] The Spirit of the Lord is upon me,

And for this anointed he me, to preach good tidings to the poor;

And he hath sent me to heal the broken-hearted,

And to proclaim forgiveness to the evil-doers, and sight to the blind,

And to bring the broken into forgiveness,

[38] And to proclaim an acceptable year of the Lord.

[39] And he rolled up the book and gave it to the servant, and went and sat down: [40] and the eyes of all that were in the synagogue were observing him. And he began to say unto them, To-day hath this scripture been fulfilled which ye have heard with [41] your ears. And they all bare him witness, and wondered at the words of grace which were proceeding from his mouth.

[42] [Arabic, p. 21] And from that time began Jesus to proclaim the gospel of the kingdom [43] of God, and to say, Repent ye, and believe in the gospel. The time is fulfilled, and the kingdom of heaven hath come near.

[44] And while he was walking on the shore of the Sea of Galilee, he saw two brethren, Simon who was called Cephas, and Andrew his brother, casting their nets into [45] the sea; for they were fishers. And Jesus said unto them, Follow me, and I will [46] make you fishers of men. And they immediately left their nets there and followed [47] him. And when he went on from thence, he saw other two brothers, James the son of Zebedee, and John his brother, in the ship with Zebedee their father, mending [48] their nets; and Jesus called them. And they immediately forsook the ship and their father Zebedee, and followed him.

[49] And when the multitude gathered unto him to hear the word of God, while he [50] was standing on the shore of the sea of Gennesaret, he saw two boats standing beside the sea, while the two fishers which were gone out of them were washing their [51] nets. And one of them belonged to Simon Cephas. And Jesus went up and sat down in it, and commanded that they should move away a little from the land into [52] the water. And he sat down

and taught the multitudes from the boat. And when he had left off his speaking, he said unto Simon, Put out into the deep, and cast your [53] net for a draught. And Simon answered and said unto him, My Master, we toiled [54] all night and caught nothing; now at thy word I will cast the net. And when they did this, there were enclosed a great many fishes; and their net was on the [55] point of breaking. And they beckoned to their comrades that were in the other boat, to come and help them. And when they came, they filled both boats, so that they were on the point of sinking.

Section VI.

[1] [Arabic, p. 22] But when Simon Cephas saw *this* he fell before the feet of Jesus, and said unto him, My Lord, I beseech of thee to depart from me, for I am [2] a sinful man. And amazement took possession of him, and of all who were with him, [3] because of the draught of the fishes which they had taken. And thus also were James and John the sons of Zebedee overtaken, who were Simon's partners. And Jesus said [4] unto Simon, Fear not; henceforth thou shalt be a fisher of men unto life. And they brought the boats to the land; and they left everything, and followed him.

[5] And after that came Jesus and his disciples into the land of Judæa; and he went [6] about there with them, and baptized. And John also was baptizing in Ænon, which is beside Salim, because there was much water there: and they came, and were baptized. [7, 8] And John was not yet come into prison. And there was an inquiry between [9] one of John's disciples and one of the Jews about purifying. And they came unto John, and said unto him, Our master, he that was with thee beyond Jordan, to

whom [10] thou hast borne witness, behold, he also baptizes, and many come to him. John answered and said unto them, A man can receive nothing of himself, except it be [11] given him from heaven. Ye are they that bear witness unto me that I said, I am [12] not the Messiah, but I am one sent before him. And he that hath a bride is a bridegroom: and the friend of the bridegroom is he that stands and listens to him, and rejoices greatly because of the bridegroom's voice. Lo now, behold, [13, 14] [Arabic, p. 23] my joy becomes complete. And he must increase and I decrease. For he that is come from above is higher than everything; and he that is of the earth, of the earth he is, and of the earth he speaks; and he that came down from heaven is [15] higher than all. And he bears witness of what he hath seen and heard: and no man [16] receives his witness. And he that hath received his witness hath asserted that he is [17] truly God. And he whom God hath sent speaks the words of God: God gave [18] not the Spirit by measure. The Father loves the Son, and hath put everything in [19] his hands. Whosoever believes in the Son has eternal life; but whosoever obeys not the Son shall not see life, but the wrath of God comes upon him.

[20] And Jesus learned that the Pharisees had heard that he had received many disciples, [21] and that he was baptizing more than John (not that Jesus was himself baptizing, [22] but his disciples); and *so* he left Judæa.

[23] And Herod the governor, because he used to be rebuked by John because of Herodias the wife of Philip his brother, and for all the sins which he was committing, [24] added to all that also this, that he shut up John in prison.

[25] And when Jesus heard that John was delivered up, he went away to Galilee. [26] And he entered again into Cana, where he had made the water wine. And there [27] was at Capernaum a king's servant, whose son was sick. And this *man* heard that Jesus was come from Judæa to Galilee; and he went to him, and besought of him that he would come down and heal his son; for he had come near unto death. [28, 29] Jesus said unto him, Except ye see signs and wonders, ye do not believe. The [Arabic, p. 24] king's servant said unto him, My Lord, come down, that the child die not. [30] Jesus said unto him, Go; for thy son is alive. And that man believed the [31] word which Jesus spoke, and went. And when he went down, his servants met him [32] and told him, and said unto him, Thy son is alive. And he asked them at what time he recovered. They said unto him, Yesterday at the seventh hour the fever left [33] him. And his father knew that that was at that hour in which Jesus said unto him, [34] Thy son is alive. And he believed, he and the whole people of his house. And this [35] is the second sign which Jesus did when he returned from Judæa to Galilee. And he was preaching in the synagogues of Galilee.

[36] And he left Nazareth, and came and dwelt in Capernaum by the sea shore, in the [37] borders of Zebulun and Naphtali: that it might be fulfilled which was said in Isaiah the prophet, who said,

[38] The land of Zebulun, the land of Naphtali,
The way of the sea, the passage of the Jordan,
Galilee of the nations:
[39] The people sitting in darkness
Saw a great light,

And those sitting in the region and in the shadow of death,

There appeared to them a light.

[40] And he taught them on the Sabbaths. And they wondered because of his doctrine: [41] for his word was as if it were authoritative. And there was in the synagogue [42] a man with an unclean devil, and he cried out with a loud voice, and said, Let me alone; what have I to do with thee, thou Jesus of Nazareth? Art thou come for our [43] destruction? I know thee who thou art, thou Holy One of God. And Jesus rebuked him, and said, Stop up thy mouth, and come out of him. And the demon threw him [44] in the midst and came out of him, having done him no harm. And great amazement [Arabic, p. 25] took hold upon every man. And they talked one with another, and said, What is this word that orders the unclean spirits with power and [45] authority, and they come out? And the news of him spread abroad in all the region which was around them.

[46] And when Jesus went out of the synagogue, he saw a man sitting among the publicans, named Matthew: and he said unto him, Come after me. And he rose, and followed him.

[47, 48] And Jesus came to the house of Simon and Andrew with James and John. And Simon's wife's mother was oppressed with a great fever, and they besought him for [49] her. And he stood over her and rebuked her fever, and it left her, and immediately [50] she rose and ministered to them. And at even they brought to him many that had [51] demons: and he cast out their devils with the word. And all that had sick, their diseases being divers *and* malignant, brought them unto him. And he laid his hand [52] on them one by one and healed

them: that that might be fulfilled which was said [53] in the prophet Isaiah, who said, He takes our pains and bears our diseases. And [54] all the city was gathered together unto the door of Jesus. And he cast out devils also from many, as they were crying out and saying, Thou art the Messiah, the Son of God; and he rebuked them. And he suffered not the demons to speak, because they knew him that he was the Lord the Messiah.

Section VII.
[1] [Arabic, p. 26] And in the morning of that day he went out very early, and went to a [2] desert place, and was there praying. And Simon and those that were with [3] him sought him. And when they found him, they said unto him, All the people seek for [4] thee. He said unto them, Let us go into the adjacent villages and towns, that I may [5] preach there also; for to this end did I come. And the multitudes were seeking him, and came till they reached him; and they took hold of him, that he should not [6] go away from them. But Jesus said unto them, I must preach of the kingdom of [7] God in other cities also: for because of this gospel was I sent. And Jesus was going about all the cities and the villages, and teaching in their synagogues, and preaching the gospel of the kingdom, and healing all the diseases and all the sicknesses, [8] and casting out the devils. And his fame became known that he was teaching in [9] every place and being glorified by every man. And when he passed by, he saw Levi the son of Alphæus sitting among the tax-gatherers; and he said unto him, Follow [10] me: and he rose and followed him. And the news of him was heard of in all the land of Syria: and they brought unto him all those whom grievous ills had befallen through divers

diseases, and those that were enduring torment, and those that were possessed, and lunatics, and paralytics; and he healed them.

[11, 12] And after some days Jesus entered into Capernaum again. And when they heard that he was in the house, many gathered, so that it could not hold them, even about [13] [Arabic, p. 27] the door; and he made known to them the word of God. And there were there some of the Pharisees and the teachers of the law, sitting, come from all the villages of Galilee, and Judæa, and Jerusalem; and the power of the Lord was [14] present to heal them. And some men brought a bed with a man on it who was paralytic. [15] And they sought to bring him in and lay him before him. And when they found no way to bring him in because of the multitude of people, they went up to the roof, and let him down with his bed from the roofing, into the midst before Jesus. [16] And when Jesus saw their faith, he said unto the paralytic, My son, thy sins are forgiven [17] thee. And the scribes and Pharisees began to think within their hearts, Why doth this man blaspheme? Who is it that is able to forgive sins, but God alone? [18] And Jesus knew by the spirit that they were thinking this within themselves, and he [19] said unto them, Why do ye think this within your heart? Which is better, that it should be said to the paralytic, Thy sins are forgiven thee, or *that* it should be said [20] to him, Arise, and take thy bed, and walk? That ye may know that the Son of man [21] is empowered on earth to forgive sins (and he said to the paralytic), I say unto thee, [22] Arise, take thy bed, and go to thine house. And he rose forthwith, and took his bed, and went out in the presence of all. And he went to his house praising God. [23] And when those multitudes saw, they feared; and

amazement took possession of [24] them, and they praised God, who had given such power to men. And they said, We have seen marvelous things to-day, of which we have never before seen the like.

[25] [Arabic, p. 28] And after that, Jesus went out, and saw a publican, named Levi, sitting [26] among the publicans: and he said unto him, Follow me. And he left [27] everything, and rose, and followed him. And Levi made him a great feast in his house. And there was a great multitude of the publicans and others sitting with him. [28] And the scribes and Pharisees murmured, and said unto his disciples, Why do ye eat [29] and drink with the publicans and sinners? Jesus answered and said unto them, The physician seeks not those who are well, but those that are afflicted with grievous [30, 31] sickness. I came not to call the righteous, but the sinners, to repentance. And they said unto him, Why do the disciples of John fast always, and pray, and the [32] Pharisees also, but thy disciples eat and drink? He said unto them, You cannot make [33] the sons of the marriage feast fast, while the bridegroom is with them. Days will come, when the bridegroom is taken away from them; then will they fast in those [34] days. And he spoke unto them a parable: No man inserts a new patch and sews it in a worn garment, lest the newness of the new take from the worn, and [35] there occur a great rent. And no man puts fresh wine into old skins, lest the wine burst the skins, and the skins be destroyed, and the wine spilled; but they put [36] the fresh wine in the new skins, and both are preserved.

And no man drinks old wine and straightway desires fresh; for he said, The old is better.

[37] And while Jesus was walking on the Sabbath day among the sown fields, his disciples [Arabic, p. 29]

hungered. And they were rubbing the ears with their hands, and [38] eating. But some of the Pharisees, when they saw them, said unto him, See, [39] why do thy disciples on the Sabbath day that which is not lawful? 580But Jesus said unto them, Have ye not read in olden time what David did, when he had need and [40] hungered, he and those that were with him? How he entered the house of God, when Abiathar was high priest, and ate the bread of the table of the Lord, which it was not lawful that any should eat, save the priests, and gave to them that were with him also? [41] And he said unto them, The Sabbath was created because of man, and man was not [42] created because of the Sabbath. Or have ye not read in the law, that the priests in [43] the temple profane the Sabbath, and *yet* they are blameless? I say unto you now, [44] that here is what is greater than the temple. If ye had known *this*: I love mercy, [45] not sacrifice, you would not have condemned those on whom is no blame. The [46] Lord of the Sabbath is the Son of man. And his relatives heard, and went out to take him, and said, He hath gone out of his mind.

[47] And on the next Sabbath day he entered into the synagogue and was teaching. [48] And there was there a man whose right hand was withered. And the scribes and the Pharisees were watching him, whether he would heal on the Sabbath day, [49] that they might find the means of accusing him. But he knew their thoughts, and said unto the man whose hand was withered, Rise and come near into the midst of [50] the synagogue. And when he came and stood, Jesus said unto them, I ask you, which is lawful to be done on the Sabbath day, good or evil? Shall lives be saved or [51] [Arabic, p. 30]

destroyed? But they were silent. Regarding them with anger, being grieved because of the hardness of their hearts. And he said unto the man, Stretch out thy hand. And he stretched it out: and his hand became straight. [52] Then he said unto them, What man of you shall have one sheep, and if it fall into a [53] well on the Sabbath day, will not take it and lift it out? And how much is man better than a sheep! Wherefore it is lawful on the Sabbath to do good.

Section VIII.

[1] And the Pharisees went out, and consulted together concerning him, that they [2] might destroy him. And Jesus perceived, and removed thence: and great multitudes [3] followed him; and he healed all of them: and he forbade them that they should [4] not make him known: that the saying in Isaiah the prophet might be fulfilled, which said,

[5] Behold, my servant with whom I am pleased;
My beloved in whom my soul hath delighted:
My spirit have I put upon him,
And he shall proclaim to the nations judgement.
[6] He shall not dispute, nor cry out;
And no man shall hear his voice in the marketplace.
[7] And a bruised reed shall he not break,
And a smoking lamp shall he not extinguish,
Until he shall bring forth judgement unto victory.
[8] And the nations shall rejoice in his name.

[9] And in those days Jesus went out to the mountain that he might pray, and he [10] spent the night there in prayer to God. And when the morning was come, he called the disciples. And

he went towards the sea: and there followed him much people
[11] from Galilee that he might pray, and from Judæa, and from Jerusalem, and from Idumæa, and from beyond Jordan, and from Tyre, and from Sidon, and from Decapolis; [12] and great multitudes came unto him, which had heard what he did. And he spoke to his disciples to bring him the boat because of the multitudes, that they [13] might not throng him. And he healed many, so that they were almost falling on [Arabic, p. 31] him on account of their seeking to get near him. And those that had [14] plagues and unclean spirits, as soon as they beheld him, would fall, and [15] cry out, and say, Thou art the Son of God. And he rebuked them much, that they [16] should not make him known. And those that were under the constraint of unclean [17] spirits were healed. And all of the crowd were seeking to come near him; because power went out from him, and he healed them all.

[18, 19] And when Jesus saw the multitudes, he went up to the mountain. And he called his disciples, and chose from them twelve; and they are those whom he named [20] apostles: Simon, whom he named Cephas, and Andrew his brother, and James and [21] John, and Philip and Bartholomew, and Matthew and Thomas, and James the son [22] of Alphæus, and Simon which *was* called the Zealot, and Judas the son of James, [23] and Judas the Iscariot, being he that had betrayed him. And Jesus went down with them and stood in the plain, and the company of his disciples, and the great [24] multitude of people. And these twelve he chose to be with him, and that he might [25] send them to preach, and to have power to heal the sick and to cast out devils.

[26] Then he lifted up his eyes unto them, and opened his mouth, and taught them, and said,

[27] Blessed are the poor in spirit: for the kingdom of heaven is theirs.

[28] Blessed are the sorrowful: for they shall be comforted.

[29] Blessed are the humble: for they shall inherit the earth.

[30] Blessed are they that hunger and thirst after righteousness: for they shall be satisfied.

[31] Blessed are the merciful: for on them shall be mercy.

[32] [Arabic, p. 32] Blessed are the pure in their hearts: for they shall see God.

[33] Blessed are the peacemakers: for they shall be called the sons of God.

[34] Blessed are they that were persecuted for righteousness' sake: for the kingdom of heaven is theirs.

[35] Blessed are ye when men shall hate you, and separate you from them, and persecute you, and reproach you, and shall speak against you with all evil talk, for my [36] sake, falsely. Then rejoice and be glad, for your reward is great in heaven: for so persecuted they the prophets before you.

[37] But woe unto you rich! For ye have received your consolation.

[38] Woe unto you that are satisfied! You shall hunger.

Woe unto you that laugh now! You shall weep and be sad.

[39] Woe unto you when men praise you! For so did their fathers use to do to the false prophets.

[40] Unto you do I say, *ye* which hear, You are the salt of the earth: if then the salt become tasteless, wherewith shall it be salted? For any purpose it is of no use, but [41] is thrown outside, and men tread upon it. Ye are the light of the world. It is [42] impossible that a city built on a mountain should be hid. Neither do they light a lamp and place it under a bushel, but on the lamp-stand, and it giveth light to all [43] who are in the house. So shall your light shine before men, that they may see [44] your good works, and glorify your Father which is in heaven. There is nothing [45] secret that shall not be revealed, or hidden that shall not be known. Whoever hath ears that hear, let him hear.

[46] Think not that I came to destroy the law or the prophets; I came not to destroy, [47] but to complete. Verily I say unto you, Until heaven and earth shall pass, there [Arabic, p. 33] shall not pass one point or one letter of the law, until all of it shall be [48] *accomplished*. Everyone who shall violate now one of these small commandments, and shall teach men so, shall be called lacking in the kingdom of heaven: everyone that shall do and teach shall be called great in the kingdom [49] of heaven. I say unto you now, unless your righteousness abound more than that of the scribes and Pharisees, ye shall not enter the kingdom of heaven.

[50] Ye have heard that it was said to the ancients, Do not kill; and every one that [51] kills is worthy of the judgement. But I say unto you that everyone who is angry with his brother without a cause is worthy of the judgement; and every one that said to his brother, Thou foul one, is condemned by the synagogue; and whosoever [52] said to him, Thou fool, is worthy of the fire of Gehenna. If thou art now offering thy gift at the altar, and

remembers there that thy brother hath conceived [53] against thee any grudge, leave thy gift at the altar, and go first and satisfy thy [54] brother, and then return and offer thy gift. Join thine adversary quickly, and while thou art still with him in the way, give a ransom and free thyself from him; [55] lest thine adversary deliver thee to the judge, and the judge deliver thee to the tax-collector, [56] and thou fall into prison. And verily I say unto thee, Thou shalt not go out thence until thou pays the last farthing.

[57, 58] Ye have heard that it was said, Do not commit adultery: but I now say unto you, that everyone that looks at a woman lusting after her hath forthwith already [59] [Arabic, p. 34] committed adultery with her in his heart. If thy right eye injure thee, put it out and cast it from thee; for it is preferable for thee that one of thy [60] members should perish, and not thy whole body go into the fire *of hell*. And if thy right hand injure thee, cut it off and cast it from thee; and it is better for thee that [61] one of thy members should perish, and not thy whole body fall into Gehenna. It was said that he that puts away his wife *should* give her a writing of divorcement: [62] but I say unto you, that everyone that puts away his wife, except for the cause of adultery, hath made it lawful for her to commit adultery: and whosoever takes one that is put away commits adultery.

Section IX.

[1] Ye have heard also that it was said unto the ancients, Lie not, but perform unto [2] God in thy oaths: but I say unto you, Swear not at all; neither by heaven, for it [3] is God's throne; nor by the earth, for it is a footstool under his feet; nor yet by [4] Jerusalem, for it is the city of the great King. Neither shalt thou swear by thy [5] head,

for thou canst not make in it one lock of hair black or white. But your word shall be either Yea or Nay, and what is in excess of this is of the evil one.

[6, 7] Ye have heard that it was said, Eye for eye, and tooth for tooth: but I say unto you, Stand not in opposition to the evil; but whosoever smites thee on thy right [8] cheek, turn to him also the other. And he that would sue thee, and take thy tunic, [9] leave to him also thy wrapper. And whosoever compels thee one mile, go with [10] [Arabic, p. 35] him twain. And he that asks thee, give unto him: and he that would borrow of thee, prevent him not. And prosecute not him that taketh thy [11] substance. And as ye desire that men should do to you, so do you also to them.

[12, 13] Ye have heard that it was said, Love thy neighbor and hate thine enemy: but I say unto you, Love your enemies, and pray for those that curse you, and deal well with those that hate you, and pray for those who take you with violence and persecute you; [14] that ye may be sons of your heavenly Father, who makes his sun to rise on the good and the evil, and sends down his rain on the righteous and the [15] unrighteous. If ye love them that love you, what reward shall ye have? For the publicans [16] and sinners also love those that love them. And if ye do a kindness to those [17] who treat you well, where is your superiority? For sinners also do likewise. And if ye lend to him of whom ye hope for a reward, where is your superiority? For the [18] sinners also lend to sinners, seeking recompense from them. But love your enemies, and do good to them, and lend, and cut not off the hope of any man; that your reward may be great, and ye may be the children of the Highest: for he is lenient [19] towards the wicked and the ungrateful. Be ye merciful, even as

your Father also is [20] merciful. And if ye inquire for the good of your brethren only, what more have [21] ye done *than others?* Is not this the conduct of the publicans also? Be perfect, even as your Father which is in heaven is perfect.

[22] Consider your alms; do them not before men to let them see you: and if it be not [23] so, ye have no reward before your Father which is in the heavens. When then thou gives an alms now, do not sound a trumpet before thee, as do the people of hypocrisy, [Arabic, p. 36] in the synagogues and the marketplaces, that men may praise them. And [24] verily say I unto you, They have received their reward. But thou, when [25] thou does alms, let thy left hand not know what thy right hand doeth; that thine alms may be concealed: and thy Father which sees in secret shall reward thee openly.

[26] And whenever thou prays, be not as the hypocrites, who love to stand in the synagogues and in the corners of the marketplaces for prayers, that men may behold [27] them. And verily say I unto you, They have received their reward. But thou, when thou prays, enter into thy closet, and fasten thy door, and pray to thy Father in secret, and thy Father which sees in secret shall reward thee openly. [28] And whenever ye pray, be not babblers, as the heathen; for they think that by the [29] abundance of their words they shall be heard. Then be not ye now like unto them: [30] for your Father knows your request before ye ask him. One of his disciples said [31] unto him, Our Lord, teach us to pray, as John taught his disciples. Jesus said unto [32] them, Thus now pray you now: Our Father which art in heaven, Hallowed be thy [33, 34] name. Thy kingdom come. Thy will be *done*, as in heaven, so on earth. Give us the [35] food of to-day.

And forgive us our trespasses, as we forgave those that trespass*ed* [36] against us. And bring us not into temptations, but deliver us from the evil one. For [37] thine is the kingdom, and the power, and the glory, for ever and ever. If ye forgive [Arabic, p. 37] men their wrong-doing, your Father which is in heaven will forgive you. [38] But if ye forgive not men, neither will your Father pardon your wrong-doing.

[39] When ye fast, do not frown, as the hypocrites; for they make their faces austere, that they may be seen of men that they are fasting. Verily I say unto you, They [40] have received their reward. But when thou fastest, wash thy face and anoint thy [41] head; that thou make not an appearance to men of fasting, but to thy Father which is in secret: and thy Father which sees in secret shall reward thee.

[42] Be not agitated, little flock; for your Father hath delighted to give you the kingdom. [43] Sell your possessions, and give in alms; take to yourselves purses that wax [44] not old. Lay not up treasure on earth, where moth and worm corrupt, and where [45] thieves break through and steal: but lay up for yourselves treasure in heaven, where [46] moth and worm do not corrupt, nor thieves break through nor steal: for where your [47] treasure is, there also will your heart be. The lamp of the body is the eye: if then [48] thine eye now be sound, thy whole body also shall be light. But if thine eye be evil, all thy body shall be dark. And if the light which is in thee is darkness, how [49] great is thy darkness! Be watchful that the light which is in thee be not darkness. [50] Because that, if thy whole body is light, and have no part dark, it shall all be light, as the lamp giveth light to thee with its flame.

Section X.

[1] [Arabic, p. 38] No man can serve two masters; and that because it is necessary that he hate one of them and love the other, and honor one of them and despise the [2] other. Ye cannot serve God and possessions. And because of this I say unto you, Be not anxious for yourselves, what you shall eat and what you shall drink; neither for your bodies, what you put on. Is not the life better than the food, and the body [3] than the raiment? Consider the birds of the heaven, which sow not, nor reap, nor store in barns; and *yet* your Father which is in heaven feeds them. Are not ye [4] better than they? Who of you when he tries is able to add to his stature one [5] cubit? If then ye are not able for a small *thing*, why are ye anxious about the [6, 7] rest? Consider the wild lily, how it grows, although it toils not, nor spins; and I say unto you that Solomon in the greatness of his glory was not clothed like one of [8] them. And if God so clothe the grass of the field, which to-day is, and to-morrow [9] is cast into the oven, how much more shall be unto you, O ye of little faith! Be not anxious, so as to say, What shall we eat? Or, What shall we drink? Or, With [10] what shall we be clothed? Neither let your minds be perplexed in this: all these *things* the nations of the world seek; and your Father which is in heaven knows [11] your need of all these things. Seek ye first the kingdom of God, and his righteousness; [12] [Arabic, p. 39] and all these shall come to you as something additional for you. Be not anxious for the morrow; for the morrow shall be anxious for what belongs to it. Sufficient unto the day is its evil.

[13] Judge not, that you be not judged: condemn not, that you be not condemned: [14] forgive, *and* it shall

be forgiven you: release, and you shall be released: give, that you may be given *unto*; with good measure, abundant, full, they shall thrust into your [15] bosoms. With what measure ye measure it shall be measured to you. See *to it* what ye hear: with what measure ye measure it shall be measured to you; and ye [16] shall be given more. I say unto those that hear, He that hath shall be given *unto*; and he that hath not, that which he regards as his shall be taken from him.

[17] And he spoke unto them a parable, Can a blind man haply guide a blind man? [18] Shall they not both fall into a hollow? A disciple is not better than his master; [19] every perfect man shall be as his master. Why look at the mote which is in the eye of your brother, but consider not the column that is in thine *own* eye? [20] Or how can you say to your brother, Brother, I will take out the mote from your eye; and the column which is in your eye you cannot see? You hypocrite, take out first the column from your eye; and then you shalt see to take out the mote from the eye of your brother.

[21] Give not that which is holy unto the dogs, neither cast your pearls before the swine, lest they trample them with their feet, and return and wound you.

[22] And he said unto them, Who of you, that hath a friend, goes to him at midnight, [23] and say unto him, My friend, lend me three loaves; for a friend hath come [24] to me from a journey, and I have nothing to offer to him: and that friend shall [Arabic, p. 40] answer him from within, and say unto him, Trouble me not; for the door is shut, and my children are with me in bed, and I cannot rise and give thee? [25] And verily I say unto you, If he will not give him because of friendship, yet because [26] of *his* importunity he will rise and give him what he

seeks. And I also say unto you, Ask, *and* ye shall be given *unto*; seek, *and* ye shall find; knock, *and* it shall be [27] opened unto you. Everyone that asks receives, and he that seeks finds, and [28] he that knocks, it shall be opened to him. What father of you, shall his son ask for bread—will he, think you, give him a stone? And if he ask of him a fish, will he, [29] think you, instead of the fish give him a serpent? And if he ask him for an egg, will [30] he, think you, extend to him a scorpion? If ye then, *although* being evil, know the gifts *which are* good, and give them to your children, how much more shall your [31] Father which is in heaven give the Holy Spirit to them that ask him? Whatsoever ye would that men should do to you, do ye even so to them: this is the law and the prophets.

[32] Enter ye by the narrow gate; for the wide gate and the broad way lead to destruction, [33] and many they be which go therein. How narrow is the gate and straitened the way leading to life! And few be they that find it.

[34] Beware of false prophets, which come to you in sheep's clothing, while within [35] they are ravening wolves. But by their fruits ye shall know them. For every tree is known by its fruit. For figs are not gathered of thorns, neither are grapes plucked of [36] briers. Even so every good tree brings forth good fruit, but the evil tree brings [37] [Arabic, p. 41] forth evil fruit. The good tree cannot bring forth evil fruit, neither *can* the [38] evil tree bring forth good fruit. The good man from the good treasures that are in his heart brings forth good *things*; and the evil man from the evil treasures that are in his heart brings forth evil *things*: and from the overflowing of the [39] heart the lips speak. Every tree that bears not good fruit is cut *down* and cast [40, 41] into the fire. Therefore

by their fruits ye shall know them. Not all that say unto me, My Lord, my Lord, shall enter the kingdom of the heavens; but he that does [42] the will of my Father which is in heaven. Many shall say unto me in that day, My Lord, my Lord, did we not prophesy in thy name, and in thy name cast out [43] devils, and in thy name do many powers? Then shall I say unto them, I never [44] knew you: depart from me, ye servants of iniquity. Every man that cometh unto [45] me, and hears my sayings, and doeth them, I will shew you to what he is like: he is like the wise man which built a house, and digged and went deep, and laid the [46] foundations on a rock: and the rain came down, and the rivers overflowed, and the winds blew, and shook that house, and it fell not: for its foundation was laid on [47] rocks. And every one that hears these my words, and doeth them not, is like [48] the foolish man which built his house on sand, without foundation: and the rain descended, and the rivers overflowed, and the winds blew, and smote upon that house, and it fell: and the fall of it was great.

Section XI.

[1] [Arabic, p. 42] And when Jesus finished these sayings, the multitudes were astonished [2] at his teaching; and that because he was teaching them as one having authority, not as their scribes and the Pharisees.

[3] And when he descended from the mountain, great multitudes followed him.

[4] And when Jesus entered Capernaum, the servant of one of the chiefs was in an [5] evil case, and he was precious to him, and he was at the point of death. And he [6] heard of Jesus, and came to him with the elders of the Jews; and he besought him, and said, My

Lord, my boy is laid in the house paralyzed, and he is suffering grievous [7] torment. And the elders urgently requested of him, and said, He is worthy that [8] this should be done unto him: for he loves our people, and he also built the synagogue [9, 10] for us. Jesus said unto him, I will come and heal him. That chief answered and said, My Lord, I am not worthy that my roof should shade thee; but it suffices [11] that thou speak a word, and my lad shall be healed. And I also am a man in obedience to authority, having under my hand soldiers: and I say to this *one*, Go, and he goes; and to another, Come, and he cometh; and to my servant that he do this, [12] and he doeth *it*. And when Jesus heard that, he marveled at him, and turned and said unto the multitude that were coming with him, Verily I say unto you, I have [13] not found in Israel *the* like *of* this faith. I say unto you, that many shall come from the east and the west, and shall recline with Abraham and Isaac and Jacob [14] [Arabic, p. 43] in the kingdom of heaven: but the children of the kingdom shall be cast [15] forth into the outer darkness: and there shall be weeping and gnashing of teeth. And Jesus said to that chief, Go thy way; as thou hast believed, *so* shall it be unto thee. [16] And his lad was healed in that hour. And that chief returned to the house and found that sick servant healed.

[17] And the day after, he was going to a city called Nain, and his disciples with him, [18] and a great multitude. And when he was come near the gate of the city, he saw a crowd accompanying one *that was* dead, the only son of his mother; and his mother was a widow: and there was with her a great multitude of the people of the [19] city. And when Jesus saw her, he had compassion on her, and said unto her, Weep [20] not. And he went

and advanced to the bier, and the bearers of it stood still; and [21] he said, Young man, I say unto thee, Arise. And that dead *man* sat up and began [22] to speak; and he gave him to his mother. And fear came on all the people: and they praised God, and said, There hath risen among us a great prophet: and, God [23] hath had regard to his people. And this news concerning him spread in all Judæa, and in all the region which was about them.

[24] And when Jesus saw great multitudes surrounding him, he commanded them to [25] depart to the other side. And while they were going in the way, there came one of the scribes and said unto him, My Master, I will follow thee whithersoever thou [26] goes. Jesus said unto him, The foxes have holes, and the birds of the heaven have [27] nests; but the Son of man hath not a place in which to lay his head. And he said unto another, Follow me. And he said unto him, My Lord, suffer me first to go and [28] bury my father. Jesus said unto him, Leave the dead to bury their dead; but thou, [29] follow me and preach the kingdom of God. And another said unto him, I will follow [Arabic, p. 44] thee, my Lord; but first suffer me to go and salute my household and [30] come. Jesus said unto him, There is no one who puts his hand to the plough and looked behind him, and *yet* is fit for the kingdom of God.

[31] And he said to them on that day in the evening, Let us go over to the other side [32] of the lake; and he left the multitudes. And Jesus went up and sat in the ship, [33] he and his disciples, and there were with them other ships. And there occurred on the sea a great tempest of whirlwind and wind, and the ship was on the point of [34] sinking from the greatness of the waves. But Jesus was sleeping on a cushion in the stern of the ship;

and his disciples came and awoke him, and said unto him, Our [35] Lord, save us; lo, we perish. And he rose, and rebuked the winds and the turbulence of the water, and said to the sea, Be still, for thou art rebuked; and the wind [36] was still, and there was a great calm. And he said unto them, Why are ye thus [37] afraid? And why have ye no faith? And they feared greatly. And they marveled, and said one to another, Who, think you, is this, who commanded also the wind and the waves and the sea, and they obey him?

[38] And they departed and came to the country of the Gadarenes, which is on the [39] other side, opposite the land of Galilee. And when he went out of the ship to the land, there met him from among the tombs a man who had a devil for a long time, [40] and wore no clothes, neither dwelt in a house, but among the tombs. And no man was [Arabic, p. 45] able to bind him with chains, because any time that he was bound with chains [41] and fetters he cut the chains and loosened the fetters; and he was snatched [42] away of the devil into the desert, and no man was able to quiet him; and at all times, in the night and in the day, he would be among the tombs and in the mountains; and no man was able to pass by that way; and he would cry out and wound himself [43] with stones. And when he saw Jesus at a distance, he hastened and worshipped [44] him, and cried with a loud voice and said, What have we to do with thee, Jesus, [45] Son of the most high God? I adjure thee by God, torment me not. And Jesus commanded the unclean spirit to come out of the man: and he had *suffered*8 a long [46] time since the time when he came into captivity to it. And Jesus asked him, What is thy name? He said unto him, Legion; for there had entered into him many [47] devils. And they

besought him that he would not command them to depart into [48] the depths. And there was there a herd of many swine, feeding in the mountain, and those devils besought him to give them leave to enter the swine; and he gave [49] them leave. And the devils went out of the man and entered into the swine. And that herd hastened to the summit and fell down into the midst of the sea, about two [50] thousand, and they were choked in the water. And when the keepers saw what [51] happened, they fled, and told those in the cities and villages. And the people went out to see what had happened; and they came to Jesus, and found the man whose [Arabic, p. 46] devils had gone out, clothed, modest, seated at the feet of Jesus; and they [52] feared. And they reported what they saw, and how the man was healed who had a devil, and concerning those swine also.

Section XII.
[1] And all the multitude of the Gadarenes entreated him to depart from them, because that great fear took hold upon them.

[2, 3] But Jesus went up into the ship, and crossed, and came to his city. And that man from whom the devils went out entreated that he might stay with him; but [4] Jesus sent him away, and said unto him, Return to thy house, and make known what [5] God hath done for thee. And he went, and began to publish in Decapolis what Jesus had done for him; and they all marveled.

[6] And when Jesus had crossed in the ship to that side, a great multitude received [7] him; and they were all looking for him. And a man named Jairus, the chief of the [8] synagogue, fell before the feet of Jesus, and besought him much, and said unto him, I have an only daughter,

and she is come nigh unto death; but come and lay thy [9] hand upon her, and she shall live. And Jesus rose, and his disciples, and they followed [10] him. And there joined him a great multitude, and they pressed him.

[11, 12] And a woman, which had a flow of blood for twelve years, *had* suffered much of many physicians, and spent all that she had, and was not benefited at all, but her [13] trouble increased further. And when she heard of Jesus, she came in the thronging of [14] [Arabic, p. 47] the crowd behind him, and touched his garments; and she thought within [15] herself, If I *could* reach to touch his garments, I should live. And immediately the fountain of her blood was dried; and she felt in her body that she was healed [16] of her plague. And Jesus straightway knew within himself that power had gone out of him; and he turned to the crowd, and said, Who approached unto my garments? [17] And on their denying, all of them, Simon Cephas and those with him said unto him, Our Master, the multitudes throng thee and press thee, and says thou, Who approached [18] unto me? And he said, Someone approached unto me; and I knew that [19] power went forth from me. And that woman, when she saw that she was not hid [20] from him, came fearing and agitated (for she knew what had happened to her), and fell down and worshipped him, and told, in the presence of all the people, for what [21] reason she touched *him*, and how she was healed immediately. And Jesus said unto her, Be of good courage, daughter; thy faith hath made thee alive; depart in peace, and be whole from thy plague.

[22] And while he was yet speaking, there came a man from the house of the chief of the synagogue, and said unto him, Thy daughter hath died; so trouble not the [23] teacher. But Jesus heard, and said unto the father of

the maid, Fear not: but believe [24] only, and she shall live. And he suffered no man to go with him, except [25] Simon Cephas, and James, and John the brother of James. And they reached the house of the chief of the synagogue; and he saw them agitated, weeping and wailing. [26] And he entered, and said unto them, Why are ye agitated *and* weeping? The [27] [Arabic, p. 48] maid hath not died, but she is sleeping. And they laughed at him, for [28] they knew that she had died. And he put every man forth without, and took the father of the maid, and her mother, and Simon, and James, and John, and [29] entered into the place where the maid was laid. And he took hold of the hand of the maid, and said unto her, Maid, arise. And her spirit returned, and straightway [30] she arose and walked: and she was about twelve years *of age*. And he commanded [31] that there should be given to her something to eat. And her father wondered greatly: [32] and he warned them that they should tell no man what had happened. And this report spread in all that land.

[33] And when Jesus crossed over from there, there joined him two blind men, crying [34] out, and saying, Have mercy on us, *thou* son of David. And when he came to the house, those two blind men came to him: and Jesus said unto them, Believe ye [35] that I am able to do this? They said unto him, Yea, our Lord. Then he touched [36] their eyes, and said, As ye have believed, it shall be unto you. And immediately their eyes were opened. And Jesus forbade them, and said, See that no man know. [37] But they went out and published the news in all that land.

[38] And when Jesus went out, they brought to him a dumb man having a devil. [39] And on the going

out of the devil that dumb man spoke. And the multitudes marveled, and said, It was never so seen in Israel

[40] And Jesus was going about in all the cities and *in* the villages, and teaching in their synagogues, and proclaiming the good news of the kingdom, and healing every disease

[41] [Arabic, p. 49] and sickness; and many followed him. And when Jesus saw the multitudes, he had compassion on them, for they were wearied and scattered, as sheep [42] that have no shepherd. And he called his twelve disciples, and gave them power and [43] much authority over all devils and diseases; and sent them two and two, that they [44] might proclaim the kingdom of God, and *to* heal the sick. And he charged them, and said, Walk not in the way of the heathen, nor enter into the cities of the Samaritans. [45, 46] Go especially unto the sheep that are lost of the sons of Israel. And [47] when ye go, proclaim and say, The kingdom of heaven is come near. And heal the sick, and cleanse the lepers, and cast out the devils: freely ye have received, freely [48, 49] give. Get you not gold, nor silver, nor brass in your purses; and take nothing for the way, except a staff only; nor bag, nor bread; neither shall ye have two tunics, [50] nor shoes, nor staff, but be shod with sandals; for the laborer is worthy of his food. [51] And whatever city or village ye enter, inquire who is worthy in it, and there be until [52, 53] ye go out. And when ye enter into the house, ask for the peace of the house: and if the house is worthy, your peace shall come upon it; but if it is not worthy, your [54] peace shall return unto you. And whosoever shall not receive you, nor hear your sayings, when ye go out from that house, or from that village, shake off the dust [55] [Arabic, p. 50] that is under your

feet against them for a testimony. And verily I say unto you, To the land of Sodom and Gomorrah there shall be rest in the day of judgement, rather than to that city.

Section XIII.

[1] I am sending you as lambs among wolves: be ye now wise as serpents, and [2] harmless as doves. Beware of men: they shall deliver you to the councils of the [3] magistrates, and scourge you in their synagogues; and shall bring you before governors and kings for my sake, for a testimony against them and against the nations. [4] And when they deliver you up, be not anxious, nor consider beforehand, what ye [5] shall say; but ye shall be given in that hour what ye ought to speak. Ye do not [6] speak, but the Spirit of your Father speaks in you. The brother shall deliver up his brother to death, and the father his son; and the sons shall rise against their [7] parents, and put them to death. And ye shall be hated of every man because of [8] my name; but he that endures unto the end of the matter shall be saved. When they expel you from this city, flee to another. Verily I say unto you, Ye shall not finish all the cities of the people of Israel, until the Son of man come.

[9, 10] A disciple is not superior to his lord, nor a servant to his master. For it is enough then for the disciple that he be as his lord, and the servant as his master. If they have called the master of the house Beelzebul, how much more the people [11] of his house! Fear them not therefore: for there is nothing covered, that shall [12] [Arabic, p. 51] not be revealed; nor hid, that shall not be disclosed and published. What I say unto you in the darkness, speak ye in the light; and what ye have told [13] secretly in the ears in closets, let it be proclaimed on the

housetops. I say unto you now, my beloved, Be not agitated at those who kill the body, but have no power to [14] kill the soul. I will inform you whom ye shall fear: him which is able to destroy [15] soul and body in hell. Yea, I say unto you, Be afraid of him especially. Are not two sparrows sold for a farthing in a bond? And one of them shall not fall on the [16] ground without your Father. But what concerns you: even the hair of your heads [17, 18] also is numbered. Fear not therefore; ye are better than many sparrows. Every man who confesses me now before men, I also will confess him before my Father [19] which is in heaven; but whosoever denies me before men, I also will deny him before my Father which is in heaven.

[20] Think ye that I am come to cast peace into the earth? I came not to cast peace, [21] but to cast dissension. Henceforth there shall be five in one house, three of them [22] disagreeing with two, and the two with the three. The father shall become hostile to his son, and the son to his father; and the mother to her daughter, and the daughter to her mother; and the mother in law to her daughter in law, and the daughter [23] in law to her mother in law: and a man's enemies shall be the people of his house. [24] Whosoever loves father or mother better than me is not worthy of me; and whosoever [Arabic, p. 52] loves son or daughter more than his love of me is not worthy of me. [25] And every one that doth not take his cross and follow me is not worthy of [26] me. Whosoever finds his life shall lose it; and whosoever loses his life for my sake shall find it.

[27] And whosoever receives you receives me; and whosoever receives me receives [28] him that sent me. And whosoever receives a prophet in the name of a

prophet shall take a prophet's reward; and whosoever shall receive a righteous man [29] in the name of a righteous man shall take a righteous man's reward. And every one that shall give to drink to one of these least ones a drink of water only, in the name of a disciple, verily I say unto you, he shall not lose his reward.

[30] And when Jesus finished charging his twelve disciples, he removed thence to [31] teach and preach in their cities. And while they were going in the way they entered into a certain village; and a woman named Martha entertained him in her house. [32] And she had a sister named Mary, and she came and sat at the feet of our Lord, [33] and heard his sayings. But Martha was disquieted by much serving; and she came and said unto him, My Lord, gives thou no heed that my sister left me alone to [34] serve? Speak to her that she help me. Jesus answered and said unto her, Martha, [35] Martha, thou art solicitous and impatient on account of many things: but what is sought is one *thing*. But Mary hath chosen for herself a good portion, and that which shall not be taken from her.

[36] And the apostles went forth, and preached to the people that they might repent. [37] And they cast out many devils, and anointed many sick with oil, and healed them. [38, 39] And the disciples of John told him of all these things. And when John heard in [Arabic, p. 53] the prison of the doings of the Messiah, he called two of his disciples, and sent them to Jesus, and said, Art thou he that cometh, or look we for [40] another? And they came to Jesus, and said unto him, John the Baptist hath sent [41] us unto thee, and said, Art thou he that cometh, or look we for another? And in that hour he cured many of diseases, and of plagues of an evil spirit; and he gave sight [42] to many blind. Jesus answered and said unto

them, Go and tell John everything ye have seen and heard: the blind see, and the lame walk, and the lepers are cleansed, and the blind hear, and the dead rise, and the poor have the gospel preached to [43] them. And blessed is he who doubted not in me.

[44] And when John's disciples departed, Jesus began to say to the multitudes concerning John, What went ye out into the wilderness to see? A reed shaken with the [45] winds? And if not, then what went ye out to see? A man clothed in soft raiment? Behold, they that are in magnificent garments and in voluptuousness are in the abode [46] of kings. And if not, then what went ye out to see? A prophet? Yea, I say unto [47] you, and more than a prophet. This is he of whom it is written,

I am sending my messenger before thy face
To prepare the way before thee.

Section XIV.

[1] Verily I say unto you, There hath not arisen among those whom women have borne a greater than John the Baptist; but he that is little now in the kingdom of heaven is greater than he.

[2] [Arabic, p. 54] And all the people which heard, and the publicans, justified God, for [3] they had been baptized with the baptism of John. But the Pharisees and the scribes wronged the purpose of God in themselves, in that they were not baptized of [4] him. And from the days of John the Baptist until now the kingdom of heaven is [5] snatched away by violence. The law and the prophets *were* until John; and after that, the kingdom of God is preached, and all press to enter it: and they that exert themselves [6, 7] snatch it away. All the prophets and the

law until John prophesied. And if ye [8] will, then receive *it*, that he is Elijah, which is to come. Whosoever hath ears that hear [9] let him hear. Easier is the perishing of heaven and earth, than the passing away of [10] one point of the law. To whom then shall I liken the people of this generation, and [11] to whom are they like? They are like the children sitting in the market, which call to their companions, and say, We sang to you, and ye danced not; we wailed to you, [12] and ye wept not. John the Baptist came neither eating bread nor drinking wine; [13] and ye said, He hath demons: and the Son of man came eating and drinking; and ye said, Behold, a gluttonous man, and a drinker of wine, and an associate of publicans [14, 15] and sinners! And wisdom was justified of all her children. And when he said that, they came to the house. And there gathered unto him again multitudes, [16] so that they found not bread to eat. And while he was casting out a devil which was dumb, when he cast out that devil, that dumb *man* spoke. And the multitudes [17] [Arabic, p. 55] marveled. And the Pharisees, when they heard, said, This *man* doth not cast out the devils, except by Beelzebul the chief of the demons, which is in him. [18, 19] And others requested of him a sign from heaven, to tempt him. And Jesus knew their thoughts, and said unto them in parables, Every kingdom that withstands itself shall become desolate; and every house or city that disagrees with itself shall not [20] stand: and if a devil cast out a devil, he withstands himself; neither shall he be [21] able to stand, but his end shall be. Then how now shall his kingdom stand? For ye [22] said that I cast out devils by Beelzebul. And if I by Beelzebul cast out the devils, then your children, by what do they cast them out? And for this cause they shall [23] be judges against you. But if I by the

Spirit of God cast out devils, then the kingdom [24] of God is come near unto you. Or how can a man enter into the house of a valiant *man*, and seize his garments, if he do not beforehand secure himself from [25] that valiant *man?* And then will he cut off his house. But when the valiant man is [26] armed, guarding his house, his possessions are in peace. But if one come who is more valiant than he, he overcomes him, and taketh his whole armor, on which [27] he relies, and divides his spoil. Whosoever is not with me is against me; and [28] whosoever gathered not with me scattered abroad. For this reason I say unto you, [Arabic, p. 56] that all sins and blasphemies with which men blaspheme shall be forgiven [29] them: but whosoever shall blaspheme against the Holy Spirit, there is no [30] forgiveness for him forever, but he is deserving of eternal punishment: because they [31] said that he had an unclean spirit. And he said also, Everyone that speaks a word against the Son of man, it shall be forgiven him; but whosoever speaks against the Holy Spirit, it shall not be forgiven him, neither in this world, nor in the world to [32] come. Either ye must make a good tree and its fruit good; or ye must make an evil [33] tree and its fruit evil: for the tree is known by its fruit. Ye children of vipers, how can ye, being evil, speak good things? From the overflowing of the heart the mouth [34] speaks. The good man from the good treasures which are in his heart brings forth good things; and the wicked man from the evil treasures which are in his [35] heart brings forth evils. I say unto you, that every idle word which men shall [36] speak, they shall give an answer for in the day of judgement: for by thy sayings thou shalt be justified, and by thy sayings thou shalt be judged.

[37] And he said to the multitudes, When ye see the clouds appear from the west, [38] straightway ye say that there cometh rain; and so it cometh to pass. And when [39] the south wind blows, ye say that there will be heat; and it cometh to pass. And when the evening is come, ye say, It *will be* fair weather, for the heaven has become [40] red. And in the morning ye say, To-day there will be severe weather, for the redness [Arabic, p. 57] of the heaven is paling. *Ye* hypocrites, ye know to examine the face of the heaven and the earth; but the signs of this time ye know not to discern.

[41] Then they brought to him one possessed of a demon, dumb *and* blind; and he [42] healed him, so that the dumb and blind began to speak and see. And all the multitudes wondered, and said, Is this, think you, the son of David?

[43] And the apostles returned unto Jesus, and told him everything that they had [44] done and wrought. And he said unto them, Come, let us go into the desert alone, and rest ye a little. And many were going and returning, and they had not leisure, not even to eat bread.

[45] And after that, there came to *him* one of the Pharisees, and besought him that he would eat bread with him. And he entered into the house of that Pharisee, and [46] reclined. And there was in that city a woman *that was* a sinner; and when she knew that he was sitting in the house of that Pharisee, she took a box of sweet ointment, [47] and stood behind him, towards his feet, weeping, and began to wet his feet with her tears, and to wipe them with the hair of her head, and to kiss his feet, and [48] anoint them with the sweet ointment. And when that Pharisee saw *it*, who invited him, he thought within himself, and said, This *man*, if he were a prophet, would

know who she is and what is her history: for the woman which touched him was a sinner.

Section XV.

[1] Jesus answered and said unto him, Simon, I have something to say unto thee. And [2] he said unto him, Say *on*, my Master. Jesus said unto him, There were two debtors [Arabic, p. 58] to one creditor; and one of them owed five hundred pence, and the other [3] owed fifty pence. And because they had not wherewith to pay, he forgave [4] them both. Which of them ought to love him more? Simon answered and said, I suppose, he to whom he forgave most. Jesus said unto him, Thou hast judged rightly. [5] And he turned to that woman, and said to Simon, Does thou see this woman? I entered into thy dwelling, and thou gives me not water to wash my feet: but this [6] *woman* hath bathed my feet with her tears, and dried them with her hair. And thou kisses me not: but this *woman*, since she entered, hath not ceased to kiss my [7] feet. And thou anointed not my head with oil: but this *woman* hath anointed [8] my feet with sweet ointment. And for this, I say unto thee, Her many sins are forgiven her, because she loved much; for he to whom little is forgiven loves little. [9, 10] And he said unto that woman, Thy sins are forgiven thee. And those that were invited [11] began to say within themselves, Who is this that forgives sins also? And Jesus said to that woman, Thy faith hath saved thee; go in peace.

[12] And many believed in him when they saw the signs which he was doing. [13, 14] But Jesus did not trust himself to them, for he knew every man, and he needed not any man to testify to him concerning every man; for he knew what was in man.

[15] And after that, Jesus set apart from his disciples other seventy, and sent them two and two before his face to every region and city whither he was purposing to [16] go. And he said unto them, The harvest is abundant, and the laborers are few: [17] entreat now the Lord of the harvest, that he send forth laborers into his harvest. Go [18] [Arabic, p. 59] ye: and lo, I am sending you as lambs among wolves. Take not with you [19] purses, nor a wallet, nor shoes; neither salute any man in the way. And [20] whatsoever house ye enter, first salute that house: and if there be there a son of peace, [21] let your peace rest upon him; but if there be not, your peace shall return to you. And be ye in that house eating and drinking what they have: for the laborer is worthy of [22] his hire. And remove not from house to house. And into whatsoever city ye enter, [23] and they receive you, eat what is presented to you: and heal the sick that are [24] therein, and say unto them, The kingdom of God is come near unto you. But whatsoever city ye enter, and they receive you not, go out into the market, and say, [25] Even the dust that clave to our feet from your city, we shake off against you; but [26] know this, that the kingdom of God is come near unto you. I say unto you, that for Sodom there shall be quiet in the day of judgement, but there shall not be for [27] that city. Then began Jesus to rebuke the cities in which there had been many [28] mighty works, and they repented not. And he said, Woe unto thee, Chorazin! Woe unto thee, Bethsaida! If there had been in Tyre and Sidon the signs which were in [29] thee, it may be that they would have repented in sackcloth and ashes. Howbeit I say unto you, that for Tyre and Sidon there shall be rest in the day of judgement, [30] more than for you. And thou, Capernaum, which art

exalted unto heaven, shalt sink down unto Hades; for if there had been in Sodom the wonders which were [31] in thee, it would have remained until this day. And now I say unto thee, that for the land of Sodom there shall be quiet in the day of judgement, more than for thee.

[32] [Arabic, p. 60] And he said again unto his apostles, Whosoever hears you hears me; and whosoever hears me hears him that sent me: and whosoever wronged you wronged me; and whosoever wronged me wronged him that sent me.

[33] And those seventy returned with great joy, and said unto him, Our Lord, even [34] the devils also are subject unto us in thy name. He said unto them, I beheld [35] Satan fallen like lightning from heaven. Behold, I am giving you authority to tread upon serpents and scorpions, and the whole race of the enemy; and nothing shall [36] hurt you. Only ye must not rejoice that the devils are subject unto you; but be glad that your names are written in heaven.

[37] And in that hour Jesus rejoiced in the Holy Spirit, and said, I acknowledge thee, my Father, Lord of heaven and earth, that thou didst hide these things from the wise and understanding, and didst reveal them unto children: yea, my Father; so [38] was thy will. And he turned to his disciples, and said unto them, Everything hath been delivered to me of my Father: and no man knows who the Son is, save the Father; and who the Father is, save the Son, and to whomsoever the Son wills [39] to reveal *him*. Come unto me, all of you, ye *that are* wearied and bearers of burdens, [40] and I will give you rest. Bear my yoke upon you, and learn of me; for I [41] am gentle and lowly in my heart: and ye shall find rest

unto your souls. For my yoke is pleasant, and my burden is light.

[42] And while great multitudes were going with him, he turned, and said unto them, [43] Whosoever comes unto me, and hates not his father, and his mother, and his brethren, and his sisters, and his wife, and his children, and himself also, cannot [44] [Arabic, p. 61] be a disciple to me. And whosoever doth not take his cross, and follow [45] me, cannot be a disciple to me. Which of you desires to build a tower, and does not sit down first and reckon his expenses and whether he hath *enough* to [46] complete it? lest when he hath laid the foundations, and is not able to finish, all that [47] behold him laugh at him, and say, This man began to build, and was not able to [48] finish. Or what king goes to the battle to fight with another king, and doth not consider first whether he is able with ten thousand to meet him that cometh to him [49] with twenty thousand? And if he is not able, he sends unto him while he is afar [50] off, and seeks peace. So shall every man of you consider, that desires to be a disciple to me; for if he renounced not all that he hath, he cannot be a disciple to me.

Section XVI.

[1] Then answered certain of the scribes and Pharisees, that they might tempt him, [2] and said, Teacher, we desire to see a sign from thee. He answered and said, This evil and adulterous generation seeks a sign; and it shall not be given a sign, [3] except the sign of Jonah the prophet. And as Jonah was a sign to the inhabitants [4] of Nineveh, so shall the Son of man also be to this generation. And as Jonah was in the belly of the great fish three days and three nights, so shall the Son of

man [5] be in the heart of the earth three days and three nights. The queen of the south shall rise in the judgement with the people of this generation, and condemn them: for she came from the ends of the earth that she might hear the Wisdom of Solomon; [6] [Arabic, p. 62] and behold, here is a better than Solomon. The men of Nineveh shall stand in the judgement with this generation, and condemn it: for they repented at [7] the preaching of Jonah; and behold, here is a greater than Jonah. The unclean spirit, when he goes out of the man, departed, and goes about through places wherein are no waters, that he may find rest for himself; and when he finds *it* not, he [8] said, I will return to my house whence I came out. And if he come and find it [9] adorned *and* set in order, then he goes, and associates with himself seven other spirits worse than himself; and they enter and dwell in it: and the end of that man [10] shall be worse than his beginning. Thus shall it be unto this evil generation.

[11] And while he was saying that, a woman from the multitude lifted up her voice, and said unto him, Blessed is the womb that bare thee, and the breasts that nursed [12] thee. But he said unto her, Blessed is he that hears the word of God, and keeps it.

[13] And while he was speaking unto the multitude, there came unto him his mother [14] and his brethren, and sought to speak with him; and they were not able, because of [15] the multitude; and they stood without and sent, calling him unto them. A man said unto him, Behold, thy mother and thy brethren *are* standing without, and seek to [16] speak with thee. But he answered unto him that spoke unto him, Who is my [17] mother? And who are my brethren? And he beckoned with his hand, stretching it out towards his disciples, and

said, Behold, my mother! And behold, my brethren! [18] And every man that shall do the will of my Father which is in heaven is my brother, and my sister, and my mother.

[19] And after that, Jesus was going about in the cities and in the villages, and proclaiming [Arabic, p. 63] and preaching the kingdom of God, and his twelve with him, [20] and the women which had been healed of diseases and of evil spirits, Mary [21] that *was* called Magdalene, from whom he had cast out seven devils, and Joanna the wife of Chuza Herod's steward, and Susanna, and many others, who were ministering to them of their substance.

[22] And after that, Jesus went out of the house, and sat on the sea shore. And there [23] gathered unto him great multitudes. And when the press of the people was great upon him, he went up and sat in the boat; and all the multitude was standing on the [24] shore of the sea. And he spoke to them much in parables, and said, The sower [25] went forth to sow: and when he sowed, some fell on the beaten highway; and it was [26] trodden upon, and the birds ate it. And other fell on the rocks: and some, where there was not much earth; and straightway it sprang up, because it had no depth in [27] the earth: and when the sun rose, it withered; and because it had no root, it dried [28] up. And some fell among thorns; and the thorns sprang up with it, and choked it; [29] and it yielded no fruit. And other fell into excellent *and* good ground; and it came up, and grew, and brought forth fruit, some thirty, and some sixty, and some [30] a hundred. And when he said that, he cried, He that hath ears that hear, let him [31] hear. And when they were alone, his disciples came, and asked him, and said unto [32] him, What is this parable? And why speaks thou unto them in parables? He [Arabic,

p. 64] answered and said unto them, Unto you is given the knowledge of the secrets of the kingdom of God; but it is not given unto them that are [33] without. He that hath shall be given unto, and there shall be added; and he that [34] hath not, that which he hath shall be taken from him also. For this *cause* therefore I speak unto them in parables; because they see, and see not; and hear, and hear [35] not, nor understand. And in them is being fulfilled the prophecy of Isaiah, who said,

>Hearing they shall hear, and shall not understand;
>And seeing they shall see, and shall not perceive:
>[36] The heart of this people is waxed gross,
>And their hearing with their ears is become heavy,
>And they have closed their eyes;
>Lest they should see with their eyes,
>And hear with their ears,
>And understand with their hearts,
>And should return,
>And I should heal them.

[37, 38] But ye, blessed are your eyes, which see; and your ears, which hear. Blessed [39] are the eyes which see what ye see. Verily I say unto you, Many of the prophets and the righteous longed to see what ye see, and saw not; and to hear what ye [40] hear, and heard not. When ye know not this parable, how shall ye know all parables? [41, 42] Hear ye the parable of the sower. The sower which sowed, sowed the word [43] of God. Everyone who hears the word of the kingdom, and understands it not, the evil one comes and snatched away the word *that hath been* sown in his [44] heart: and this is that *which was* sown on the middle of the highway. But *that* which was sown on the rocks is he that hears the word, and straightway receives [45, 46] [Arabic, p. 65] it

with joy; only, it hath no root in his soul, but his belief in it *is* for a time; and whenever there is distress or persecution because of a word, he [47] stumbles quickly. And *that which was* sown among the thorns is he that hears the word; and the care of this world, and the error of riches, and the rest of the [48] other lusts enter, and choke the word, and it becomes without fruit. And that which was sown in good ground is he that hears my word in a pure *and* good heart, and understands it, and holds to it, and brings forth fruit with patience, and produces either a hundredfold or sixtyfold or thirty.

[49] And he said, So is the kingdom of God, like a man who casted seed into the [50] earth, and slept and rises by night and day, and the seed grows and comes [51] up, whence he knows not. And the earth brings it to the fruit; and first it [52] will be blade, and after it ear, and at last perfect wheat in the ear: and whenever the fruit ripened, he brings immediately the sickle, for the harvest hath come.

Section XVII.

[1] And he set forth to them another parable, and said, The kingdom of heaven is [2] like a man who sowed good seed in his field; but when men slept, his enemy came [3] and sowed tares among the wheat, and went away. And when the blade sprang up [4] and brought forth fruit, there were noticed the tares also. And the servants of the master of the house came, and said unto him, Our lord, didst thou not sow good [5] [Arabic, p. 66] seed in thy field? Whence are there tares in it? He said unto them, An enemy hath done this. His servants said unto him, Wilt thou that we go [6] and separate it? He said unto them, Perhaps, when ye separate the tares, ye

would [7] root up with them wheat also. Leave them to grow both together until the harvest: and in the time of the harvest I will say unto the reapers, Separate the tares first, and bind them in bundles to be burned with fire; and gather the wheat into my barns.

[8, 9] And he set forth to them another parable, and said, To what is the kingdom of [10] God like? And to what shall I liken it? And in what parable shall I set it forth? It [11] is like a grain of mustard seed, which a man took, and planted in his field: and of the number of the things that are sown in the earth it is smaller than all of the things [12] which are sown, which are upon the earth; but when it is grown, it is greater than all the herbs, and produces large branches, so that the birds of heaven make *their* nests in its branches.

[13, 14] And he set forth to them another parable: To what shall I liken the kingdom of [15] God? It is like the leaven which a woman took, and kneaded into three measures of flour, until the whole of it was leavened.

[16] And Jesus spoke all that to the multitudes by way of parables, according as they [17] were able to hear. And without parables spoke he not unto them; that the saying of the Lord through the prophet might be fulfilled:

I will open my mouth in parables;

And I will utter secrets which were before the foundations of the world.

[18] But he explained to his disciples privately everything.

[19] Then Jesus left the multitudes, and came to the house. And his disciples came unto him, and said unto him, Explain unto us that parable about the tares [20] [Arabic, p. 67] and the field. He answered and said unto

them, He that sowed good seed is [21] the Son of man; and the field is the world; and the good seed are the children of the [22] kingdom; and the tares are the children of the evil one; and the enemy that sowed them is Satan; and the harvest is the end of the world; and the reapers are the angels. [23] And as the tares are separated and burned in the fire, so shall it be in the end of [24] this world. The Son of man shall send his angels, and separate from his kingdom [25] all things that injure, and all the doers of iniquity, and they shall cast them into the [26] furnace of fire: and there shall be weeping and gnashing of teeth. Then the righteous shall shine as the sun in the kingdom of their Father. Whosoever hath ears that hear, let him hear.

[27] And again the kingdom of heaven is like treasure hid in a field: that which a man found and hid; and, for his pleasure in it, went and sold all that he had, and bought that field.

[28] And again the kingdom of heaven is like a man *that is* a merchant seeking excellent [29] pearls; and when he found one pearl of great price, he went and sold everything that he had, and bought it.

[30] And again the kingdom of heaven is like a net that was cast into the sea, and [31] gathered of every kind: and when it was filled, they drew it up on to the shore of the sea, and sat down to select; and the good of them they threw into the vessels, [32] and the bad they threw outside. Thus shall it be in the end of the world: the angels [33] shall go forth, 1241and separate the wicked from among the good, and shall cast them into the furnace of fire: there shall be weeping and gnashing of teeth.

[34] Jesus said unto them, Have ye understood all these *things?* They said unto [35] [Arabic, p. 68] him,

Yea, our Lord. He said unto them, Therefore every scribe that becomes a disciple of the kingdom of heaven is like a man that is a householder, who brings out of his treasures the new and the old.

[36, 37] And when Jesus had finished all these parables, he removed thence, and came to his city; and he taught them in their synagogues, so that they were perplexed. [38] And when the Sabbath came, Jesus began to teach in the synagogue; and many of [39] those that heard marveled, and said, Whence came these things to this *man?* And many envied him and gave no heed to him, but said, What is this wisdom that is given to this *man*, that there should happen at his hands such as these mighty works? [40] Is not this a carpenter, son of a carpenter? And is not his mother called Mary? And [41] his brethren, James, and Joses, and Simon, and Judas? And his sisters, all of them, [42] lo, are they not all with us? Whence hath this *man* all these things? And they were in doubt concerning him. And Jesus knew their opinion, and said unto them, Will ye haply say unto me this proverb, Physician, heal first thyself: and all that [43] we have heard that thou didst in Capernaum, do here also in thine *own* city? And he said, Verily I say unto you, A prophet is not received in his *own* city, nor among [44] his brethren: for a prophet is not despised, save in his *own* city, and among his *own* [45] kin, and in his *own* house. Verily I say unto you, In the days of Elijah the prophet, there were many widows among the children of Israel, when the heaven held back [46] three years and six months, and there was a great famine in all the land; and Elijah [Arabic, p. 69] was not sent to one of them, save to Zarephath of Sidon, to a woman that was [47] a widow. And many lepers were among the children of Israel in the

days of Elisha the prophet; but not one of them was cleansed, save Naaman the Nabathæan. [48] And he was not able to do there many mighty works, because of their unbelief; [49] except that he laid his hand upon a few of the sick, and healed *them*. And he marveled [50] at their lack of faith. And when those who were in the synagogue heard, [51] they were all filled with wrath; and they rose up, and brought him forth outside the city, and brought him to the brow of the hill upon which their city was built, that [52] they might cast him from its summit: but he passed through among them and went away.

[53] And he went about in the villages which *were* around Nazareth, and taught in their synagogues.

Section XVIII.

[1] At that time Herod the tetrarch heard of the fame of Jesus, and all the things which came to pass at his hand; and he marveled, for he had obtained excellent [2] information concerning him. And *some* men said that John the Baptist was risen [3] from among the dead; and others said that Elijah had appeared; and others, Jeremiah; [4] and others, that a prophet of the old prophets was risen; and others said that he [5] was a prophet like one of the prophets. Herod said to his servants, This is John the Baptist, he whom I beheaded; he is risen from among the dead: therefore mighty [6] [Arabic, p. 70] works result from him. For Herod him*self* had sent and taken John, and cast him into prison, for the sake of Herodias his brother Philip's wife, whom he [7] had taken. And John said to Herod, Thou hast no authority to take the wife of thy [8] brother. And Herodias avoided him and wished to kill

him; and she could not. [9] But Herod feared John, for he knew that he was a righteous man *and* a holy; and [10] he guarded him, and heard him much, and did, and obeyed him with gladness. And he wished to kill him; but he feared the people, for they adhered to him as the [11] prophet. And there was a celebrated day, and Herod had made a feast for his great men on the day of his anniversary, and for the officers and for the chief men [12] of Galilee. And the daughter of Herodias came in and danced in the midst of the company, and pleased Herod and those that sat with him. And the king said to the [13] damsel, Ask of me what thou wilt, and I will give it thee. And he swore unto her, [14] Whatsoever thou shalt ask, I will give it thee, to the half of my kingdom. And she went out, and said unto her mother, What shall I ask him? She said unto her, The [15] head of John the Baptist. And immediately she came in hastily to the king, and said unto him, I desire in this hour that thou give me on a dish the head of John [16] the Baptist. And the king was exceeding sorry; but because of the oath and the [17] guests he did not wish to refuse her. But immediately the king sent an executioner, and commanded that he should bring the head of John: and he went and cut off [18] the head of John in the prison, and brought it on a dish, and delivered it to the [19] damsel; and the damsel gave it to her mother. And his disciples heard, and came [Arabic, p. 71] and took his body, and buried it. And they came and told Jesus what [20] had happened. And for this cause Herod said, I beheaded John: who [21] is this, of whom I hear these things. And he desired to see him. And Jesus, when he heard, removed thence in a boat to a waste place alone, to the other side of the sea of the Galilee of Tiberias.

[22] And many saw them going, and knew them, and hastened by land from all the cities, and came thither beforehand; for they saw the signs which he was doing on the [23, 24] sick. And Jesus went up into the mountain, and sat there with his disciples. And [25] the feast of the Passover of the Jews was near. And Jesus lifted up his eyes, and saw great multitudes coming to him. And he was moved with compassion for them, for [26] they were like sheep that *were* without a shepherd. And he received them, and spoke to them concerning the kingdom of God, and healed those who had need of healing.

[27] And when the evening approached, his disciples came to him, and said unto [28] him, The place is desert, and the time is past; send away the multitudes of the people, that they may go to the towns and villages which are around us, and buy for [29] themselves bread; for they have nothing to eat. But he said unto them, They have [30] no need to go away; give ye them what may be eaten. They said unto him, We have not here *enough*. He said unto Philip, Whence shall we buy bread that these may eat? [31, 32] And he said that proving him; and he knew what he was resolved to do. Philip said [Arabic, p. 72] unto him, Two hundred pennyworth of bread would not suffice them after [33] every one of them hath taken a small amount. One of his disciples said unto [34] him (namely, Andrew the brother of Simon Cephas), Here is a lad having five loaves [35] of barley and two fishes: but this amount, what is it for all these? But wilt thou that we go and buy for all the people what may be eaten? For we have no more [36] than these five loaves and the two fishes. And the grass was plentiful in that place. Jesus said unto them, Arrange all the people that they may sit down on the grass, [37] fifty people in a company. And the

disciples did so. And all the people sat down [38] by companies, by hundreds and fifties. Then Jesus said unto them, Bring hither [39] those five loaves and the two fishes. And when they brought him that, Jesus took the bread and the fish, and looked to heaven, and blessed, and divided, and gave to [40] his disciples to set before them; and the disciples set for the multitudes the bread [41] and the fish; and they ate, all of them, and were satisfied. And when they were satisfied, he said unto his disciples, Gather the fragments that remain over, that nothing [42] be lost. And they gathered, and filled twelve baskets with fragments, being those that remained over from those which ate of the five barley loaves and the two [43] fishes. And those people who ate were five thousand, besides the women and children. [44] [Arabic, p. 73] And straightway he pressed his disciples to go up into the ship, and that they should go before him unto the other side to Bethsaida, while he [45] him*self* should send away the multitudes. And those people who saw the sign which [46] Jesus did, said, Of a truth this is a prophet who hath come into the world. And Jesus knew their purpose to come and take him, and make him a king; and he left them, and went up into the mountain alone for prayer.

[47, 48] And when the nightfall was near, his disciples went down unto the sea, and sat in a boat, and came to the side of Capernaum. And the darkness came on, and Jesus [49] had not come to them. And the sea was stirred up against them by reason of a violent [50] wind that blew. And the boat was distant from the land many furlongs, and they were much damaged by the waves, and the wind was against them.

Section XIX.

[1] And in the fourth watch of the night Jesus came unto them, walking upon the [2] water, after they had rowed with difficulty about twenty-five or thirty furlongs. [3] And when he drew near unto their boat, his disciples saw him walking on the water; and they were troubled, and supposed that it was a false appearance; and they cried [4] out from their fear. But Jesus straightway spoke unto them, and said, Take courage, [5] for it is I; fear not. Then Cephas answered and said unto him, My Lord, if it be thou, [6] bid me to come unto thee on the water. And Jesus said unto him, Come. And [7] Cephas went down out of the boat, and walked on the water to come unto Jesus. But [Arabic, p. 74] when he saw the wind strong, he feared, and was on the point of sinking; [8] and he lifted up his voice, and said, My Lord, save me. And immediately our Lord stretched out his hand and took *hold of* him, and said unto him, [9] Thou of little faith, why didst thou doubt? And when Jesus came near, he went up [10] unto them into the boat, he and Simon, and immediately the wind ceased. And those that were in the ship came and worshipped him, and said, Truly thou art the [11] Son of God. And straightway that ship arrived at the land which they made for. [12] And when they came out of the ship to the land, they marveled greatly and were [13] perplexed in themselves: and they had not understood by means of that bread, because their heart was gross.

[14] And when the people of that region knew of the arrival of Jesus, they made haste in all that land, and began to bring those that were diseased, borne in their [15] beds to the place where they heard that he was. And wheresoever the place *might be* which he entered, of the villages or the cities, they laid the sick in the markets, and

sought of him that they might touch were it only the edge of his garment: and all that touched him were healed and lived.

[16] And on the day after that, the multitude which was standing on the shore of the sea saw that there was there no other ship save that into which the disciples had [17] gone up, and that Jesus went not up into the ship with his disciples (but there were other ships from Tiberias near the place where they ate the bread when Jesus blessed [18] *it*): and when that multitude saw that Jesus was not there, nor yet his disciples, they [19] [Arabic, p. 75] went up into those ships, and came to Capernaum, and sought Jesus. And when they found him on the other side of the sea, they said unto him, Our [20] Master, when came you hither? Jesus answered and said unto them, Verily, verily, I say unto you, Ye have not sought me because of your seeing the signs, but because of [21] your eating the bread and being satisfied. Serve not the food which perishes, but the food which abides in eternal life, which the Son of man will give unto you: him [22] hath God the Father sealed. They said unto him, What shall we do that we may [23] work the work of God? Jesus answered and said unto them, This is the work of [24] God, that ye believe in him whom he hath sent. They said unto him, What sign hast thou done, that we may see, and believe in thee? What hast thou wrought? [25] Our fathers ate the manna in the wilderness; as it was written, Bread from heaven [26] gave he them to eat. Jesus said unto them, Verily, verily, I say unto you, Moses gave you not bread from [27] heaven; but my Father gave you the bread of truth from heaven. The bread of God is that which came down from heaven and gave the [28, 29] world life. They said unto him, Our Lord, give us at all times this

bread. Jesus said unto them, I am the bread of life: whosoever cometh unto me shall not hunger, [30] and whosoever believeth in me shall not thirst for ever. But I said unto you, [31] Ye have seen me, and have not believed. And all that my Father hath given to me cometh unto me; and whosoever cometh unto me I shall not cast him forth without. [32] came down from heaven, not to do my *own* will, but to do the will of him [33] that sent me; and this is the will of him that sent me, that I should lose nothing of [34] [Arabic, p. 76] that which he gave me, but raise it up in the last day. This is the will of my Father, that everyone that sees the Son, and believes in him, should have eternal life; and I will raise him up in the last day.

[35] The Jews therefore murmured against him because of his saying, I am the bread [36] which came down from heaven. And they said, Is not this Jesus, the son of Joseph, whose father and mother we know? Then how said this *man*, I came down from [37, 38] heaven? Jesus answered and said unto them, Murmur not one with another. No man is able to come unto me, except the Father which sent me draw him; and I will [39] raise him up in the last day. It is written in the prophet, They shall all be the taught of God. Everyone who hears from the Father now, and learns of him, comes [40] unto me. No man now sees the Father; but he that is from God, he it is that sees [41] the Father. Verily, verily, I say unto you, Whosoever believeth in me hath eternal [42, 43] life. I am the bread of life. Your fathers ate the manna in the wilderness, and [44] they died. This is the bread which came down from heaven, that a man may eat [45] of it, and not die. I am the bread of life which came down from heaven: and if a man eat of this bread he shall live

forever: and the bread which I shall give is my body, which I give for the life of the world.

[46] The Jews therefore quarreled one with another, and said, How can he give us [47] [Arabic, p. 77] his body that we may eat it? Jesus said unto them, Verily, verily, I say unto you, If ye do not eat the body of the Son of man and drink his blood, ye shall [48] not have life in yourselves. Whosoever eats of my body and drinks of my blood [49] hath eternal life; and I will raise him up in the last day. My body truly is meat, and [50] my blood truly is drink. Whosoever eats my body and drinks my blood abides [51] in me, and I in him—as the living Father sent me, and I am alive because of the [52] Father; and whosoever eats me, he also shall live because of me. This is the bread which came down from heaven: and not according as your fathers ate the [53] manna, and died: whosoever eats of this bread shall live forever. This he said in [54] the synagogue, when he was teaching in Capernaum. And many of his disciples, when they heard, said, This word is hard; who is he that can hear it?

Section XX.

[1] And Jesus knew within himself that his disciples were murmuring because of [2] that, and he said unto them, Does this trouble you? *What* if ye should see the Son [3] of man then ascend to the place where he was of old? It is the spirit that quickened, and the body profited nothing: the words that I speak unto you are spirit [4] and life. But there are some of you that do not believe. And Jesus knew beforehand who they were who should not believe, and who it was that should betray [5] him. And he said unto them, Therefore I said unto you, No

man can come unto me, if that hath not been given him by the Father.

[6] [Arabic, p. 78] And because of this word many of his disciples turned back and walked [7] not with him. And Jesus said unto the twelve, Do ye haply also wish to [8] go away? Simon Cephas answered and said, My Lord, to whom shall we go? Thou [9] hast the words of eternal life. And we have believed and known that thou art the [10] Messiah, the Son of the living God. Jesus said unto them, Did not I choose you, [11] ye company of the twelve, and of you one is a devil? He said that because of Judas the son of Simon Iscariot; for he, being of the twelve, was purposed to betray him.

[12] And while he was speaking, one of the Pharisees came asking of him that he [13] would eat with him: and he went in, and reclined *to meat*. And that Pharisee, when [14] he saw it, marveled that he had not first cleansed himself before his eating.

Jesus said unto him, Now do ye Pharisees wash the outside of the cup and the dish, and ye think that ye are cleansed; but your inside is full of injustice and wickedness.

[15, 16] Ye of little mind, did not he that made the outside make the inside? Now give what ye have in alms, and everything *shall be* clean unto you.

[17, 18] And there came to him Pharisees and scribes, come from Jerusalem. And when they saw some of his disciples eating bread while they had not washed their hands, [19] they found fault. For all of the Jews and the Pharisees, if they wash not their [20] hands thoroughly, eat not; for they held to the ordinance of the elders. And they ate not what was bought from the market, except they washed it; and many other things did

they keep of what they had received, such as the washing of cups, and [21] measures, and vessels of brass, and couches. And scribes and Pharisees asked him, [Arabic, p. 79] Why do thy disciples not walk according to the ordinances of the elders, but [22] eat bread without washing their hands? Jesus answered and said unto them, Why do ye also overstep the command of God by reason of your ordinance? [23] God said, Honor thy father and thy mother; and, Whosoever reviles his father and [24] his mother shall surely die. But ye say, If a man say to his father or to his mother, [25] What thou receives from me is an offering,—and ye suffer him not to do anything [26] for his father or his mother; and ye make void and reject the word of God by reason of the ordinance that ye have ordained and commanded, such as the washing [27] of cups and measures, and what resembles that ye do much. And ye forsook [28] the command of God, and held to the ordinance of men. Do ye well to wrong [29] the command of God in order that ye may establish your ordinance? Ye hypocrites, well did Isaiah the prophet prophesy concerning you, and say,

> [30] This people honored me with its lips;
> But their heart is very far from me.
> [31] But in vain do they fear me,
> In that they teach the commands of men.

[32] And Jesus called all the multitude, and said unto them, Hear me, all of you, and [33] understand: nothing without the man, which then enters him, is able to defile him; [34] but what goes out of him, that it is which defiles the man. He that hath ears [35] that hear, let him hear. Then his disciples drew near, and said unto him, Knows [36] thou that the Pharisees which heard this word were angry? He answered and said unto them, Every plant

which my Father which is in heaven planted not shall be [37] [Arabic, p. 80] uprooted. Let them alone; for they are blind leading blind. And if the blind lead the blind, both of them shall fall into a hollow.

[38] And when Jesus entered the house from the multitude, Simon Cephas asked him, [39] and said unto him, My Lord, explain to us that parable. He said unto them, Do ye also thus not understand? Know ye not that everything that enters into the [40] man from without cannot defile him; because it enters not into his heart; it enters into his stomach only, and thence is cast forth in the cleansing which makes [41] clean all the food? The thing which goes forth from the mouth of the man proceeded [42] from his heart, and it is that which defiles the man. From within the [43] heart of men proceed evil thoughts, fornication, adultery, theft, false witness, murder, injustice, wickedness, deceit, stupidity, evil eye, calumny, pride, foolishness: [44] these evils all of them from within proceed from the heart, and they are *the things* [45] which defile the man: but if a man eat while he washes not his hands, he is not defiled.

[46] And Jesus went out thence, and came to the borders of Tyre and Sidon. And he entered into a certain house, and desired that no man should know it; and [47] he could not be hid. But straightway a Canaanitish woman, whose daughter had an [48, 49] unclean spirit, heard of him. And that woman was a Gentile of Emesa of Syria. And she came out after him, crying out, and saying, Have mercy upon me, my Lord, *thou* [50] son of David; for my daughter is seized in an evil way by Satan. And he answered [Arabic, p. 81] her not a word. And his disciples came and besought him, and said, Send [51] her away: for she cries after us. He answered and said unto them, I was

[52] not sent except to the sheep that are gone astray of the house of Israel. But she came and worshipped him, and said, My Lord, help me, have mercy upon me.

[53] Jesus said unto her, It is not seemly that the children's bread should be taken and [54] thrown to the dogs. But she said, Yea, my Lord: the dogs also eat of the crumbs [55] that fall from their masters' tables, and live. Then said Jesus unto her, O woman, [56] great is thy faith: it shall be unto thee as thou hast desired. Go then *thy way;* and [57] because of this word, the devil is gone out of thy daughter. And her daughter was [58] healed in that hour. And that woman went away to her house, and found her daughter laid upon the bed, and the devil gone out of her.

Section XXI.

[1] And Jesus went out again from the borders of Tyre and Sidon, and came to the [2] sea of Galilee, towards the borders of Decapolis. And they brought unto him one dumb and deaf, and entreated him that he would lay his hand upon him and heal [3] him. And he drew him away from the multitude, and went away alone, and spat [4] upon his fingers, and thrust *them* into his ears, and touched his tongue; and looked [5] to heaven, and sighed, and said unto him, Be opened. And in that hour his ears [6] were opened, and the bond of his tongue was loosed, and he spoke with ease. And Jesus charged them much that they should not tell this to any man: but the more [7] he charged them, *the more* they increased in publishing, and marveled much, and [Arabic, p. 82] said, This *man* doeth everything well: he made the deaf to hear, and those that lacked speech to speak.

[8, 9] And while he was passing through the land of Samaria, he came to one of the cities of the Samaritans, called Sychar, beside the field which Jacob gave to Joseph to [10] his son. And there was there a spring of water of Jacob's. And Jesus was fatigued from the exertion of the way, and sat at the spring. And the time was about the [11] sixth hour. And a woman of Samaria came to draw water; and Jesus said unto [12] her, Give me water, that I may drink. 1491And his disciples had entered into the city [13] to buy for themselves food. And that Samaritan woman said unto him, How dost thou, being a Jew, ask me to give thee to drink, while I am a Samaritan woman? [14] (And the Jews mingle not with the Samaritans.) Jesus answered and said unto her, If thou knew the gift of God, and who this is that said unto thee, Give me [15] to drink; thou would ask him, and he would give thee the water of life. That woman said unto him, My Lord, thou hast no bucket, and the well is deep: from [16] whence hast thou the water of life? Can it be that thou art greater than our father Jacob, who gave us this well, and drank from it, and his children, and his sheep? [17] Jesus answered and said unto her, Everyone that drinks of this water shall thirst [18] again: but whosoever drinks of the water which I shall give him shall not thirst for ever: but the water which I shall give him shall be in him a spring of water springing [19] up unto eternal life. That woman said unto him, My Lord, give me of this water, that [20] I may not thirst again, neither come and draw water from here. Jesus said unto her, [21] [Arabic, p. 83] Go and call thy husband, and come hither. She said unto him, I have no [22] husband. Jesus said unto her, Thou said well, I have no husband: five husbands hast thou had, and this *man* whom thou hast now is not thy husband; and [23] in this

thou said truly. That woman said unto him, My Lord, I perceive thee to [24] be a prophet. Our fathers worshipped in this mountain; and ye say that in Jerusalem [25] is the place in which worship must be. Jesus said unto her, Woman, believe me, an hour cometh, when neither in this mountain, nor yet in Jerusalem, shall ye worship [26] the Father. Ye worship that which ye know not: but we worship that which [27] we know: for salvation is of the Jews. But an hour cometh, and now is, when the true worshippers shall worship the Father in spirit and truth: and the Father also [28] seeks such as these worshippers. For God is a Spirit: and they that worship him [29] must worship him in spirit and in truth. That woman said unto him, I know that [30] the Messiah cometh: and when he is come, he will teach us everything. Jesus said unto her, I that speak unto thee am he.

[31] And while he was speaking, his disciples came; and they wondered how he would speak with a woman; but not one of them said unto him, What seeks thou? Or, [32] What speaks thou with her? And the woman left her water pot, and went to the [33] city, and said to the people, Come, and see a man who told me all that *ever* I did: [34] perhaps then he is the Messiah. And people went out from the city, and came to [35] him. And in the mean while his disciples besought him, and said unto him, Our [36, 37] master, eat. And he said unto them, I have food to eat that ye know not. And the disciples said amongst themselves, Can anyone have brought him aught to eat? [38] Jesus said unto them, My food is to do the will of him that sent me, and to accomplish [39] [Arabic, p. 84] his work. Said ye not that after four months cometh the harvest? Behold, I therefore say unto you, Lift up your eyes, and behold the lands, [40]

that they have become white, and the harvest is already come. And he that reaped receives his wages, and gathered the fruit of eternal life; and the sower and [41] the reaper rejoice together. For in this is found the word of truth, One sowed, and [42] another reaped. And I sent you to reap that in which ye have not labored: others labored, and ye have entered on their labor.

[43] And from that city many of the Samaritans believed in him because of the words [44] of that woman, who testified and said, He told me all that *ever* I did. And when those Samaritans came unto him, they besought him to abide with them; and he [45, 46] abode with them two days. And many believed in him because of his word; and they said to that woman, Now not because of thy saying have we believed in him: we have heard and known that this truly is the Messiah, the Savior of the world.

[47, 48] And after two days Jesus went out thence and departed to Galilee. And Jesus [49] testified that a prophet is not honored in his own city. And when he came to Galilee, the Galilæans received him.

Section XXII.

[1] And when Jesus came to a certain village, there drew near to him a leper, and fell at his feet, and besought him, and said unto him, If thou wilt, thou art able to [2] cleanse me. And Jesus had mercy upon him, and stretched forth his hand, and [3] touched him, and said, I will cleanse thee. And immediately his leprosy departed [4] from him, and he was cleansed. And he sternly charged him, and sent him out, [5] [Arabic, p. 85] and said unto him, See that thou tell *not* any man: but go and shew thyself to the priests, and offer an offering for thy cleansing as Moses commanded [6] for their

testimony. But he, when he went out, began to publish much, and spread abroad the news, so that Jesus could not enter into any of the cities openly, for the extent to which the report of him spread, but he remained without in a desert [7] place. And much people came unto him from one place and another, to hear [8] his word, and that they might be healed of their pains. And he used to withdraw from them into the desert, and pray.

[9] And after that, was the feast of the Jews; and Jesus went up to Jerusalem.

[10] And there was in Jerusalem a place prepared for bathing, which was called in [11] Hebrew the House of Mercy, having five porches. And there were laid in them much people of the sick, and blind, and lame, and paralyzed, waiting for the moving [12] of the water. And the angel from time to time went down into the place of bathing, and moved the water; and the first that went down after the moving [13] of the water, every pain that he had was healed. And a man was there who had a [14] disease for thirty-eight years. And Jesus saw this *man* laid, and knew that he had [15] been thus a long time; and he said unto him, Would thou be made whole? That diseased one answered and said, Yea, my Lord, I have no man, when the water moves, to put me into the bathing-place; but when I come, another goes down before [16, 17] me. Jesus said unto him, Rise, take thy bed, and walk. And immediately that man was healed; and he rose, and carried his bed, and walked.

[18] And that day was a Sabbath. And when the Jews saw that healed one, they said [19] unto him, It is a Sabbath: thou hast no authority to carry thy bed. And he answered and said unto them, He that made me whole, the same said unto me, Take thy bed, [20] [Arabic, p. 86] and

walk. They asked him therefore, Who is this man that said unto thee, [21] Take thy bed, and walk? But he that was healed knew not who it was; for Jesus had removed from that place to another, because of the press of the great multitude [22] which was in that place. And after two days Jesus happened upon him in the temple, and said unto him, Behold, thou art whole: sin not again, lest there come upon [23] thee what is worse than the first. And that man went, and said to the Jews that it [24] was Jesus that had healed him. And because of that the Jews persecuted Jesus and [25] sought to kill him, because he was doing this on the Sabbath. And Jesus said unto [26] them, My Father works until now, and I also work. And because of this especially the Jews sought to kill him, not because he profaned the Sabbath only; but for his saying also that God was his Father, and his making himself equal with God. [27] Jesus answered and said unto them, Verily, verily, I say unto you, The Son cannot do anything of himself, but what he sees the Father do; what the Father doeth, [28] that the Son also doeth like him. The Father loves his Son, and everything that he does he shows him: and more than these works will he shew him, that ye [29] may marvel. And as the Father raises the dead and gives them life, so the Son [30] also giveth life to whomsoever he will. And the Father judges no man, but hath [31] given all judgement unto the Son; that every man may honor the Son, as he honored the Father. And he that honored not the Son honored not the Father which [32] sent him. Verily, verily, I say unto you, Whosoever hears my word, and believes in him that sent me, hath eternal life, and cometh not into judgement, but passes from [33] [Arabic, p. 87] death unto life. Verily, verily, I say unto you, An hour shall come, and now is also, when the dead shall hear the voice of the Son of God; and those [34] which hear shall live. And as the Father hath life in himself, likewise he gave to [35] the Son also that he might have life in himself, and authority to do judgement also, [36] because he is the Son of man. Marvel not then at that: I mean the coming of the hour when all that are in the tombs shall hear his voice, and shall come forth: [37] those that have done good, to the resurrection of life; and those that have done evil *deeds*, to the resurrection of judgement.

[38] I am not able of myself to do anything; but as I hear, I judge: and my judgement [39] is just; I seek not my *own* will, but the will of him that sent me. I bear witness [40] of myself, and so my witness is not true. It is another that bears witness [41] of me; and I know that the witness which he bears of me is true. Ye have sent [42] unto John, and he hath borne witness of the truth. But not from man do I seek [43] witness; but I say that ye may live. That was a lamp which shines and [44] giveth light: and ye were pleased to glory now in his light. But I have witness greater than that of John: the works which my Father hath given me to accomplish, [45] those works which I do, bear witness of me, that the Father hath sent me. And the Father which sent me, he hath borne witness of me. Ye have neither heard his [46] voice at any time, nor seen his appearance. And his word abides not in you; because [47] in him whom he hath sent ye do not believe. Search the scriptures, in which ye rejoice [48] that ye have eternal life; and they bear witness of me; and ye do not wish to come to [49, 50] [Arabic, p. 88] me, that ye may have eternal life. I seek not praise of men. But I know [51] you, that the love of God is not in you. I am come in the name of my Father, and ye received me not;

but if another come in his own name, that *one* will [52] ye receive. And how can ye believe, while ye receive praise one from another, and [53] praise from God, the One, ye seek not? Can it be that ye think that I will accuse you before the Father? Ye have one that accuses you, Moses, in whom ye have [54] rejoiced. If ye believed Moses, ye would believe me also; Moses wrote of me. [55] And if ye believed not his writings, how shall ye believe my words?

Section XXIII.

[1] And Jesus departed thence, and came to the side of the Sea of Galilee, and went [2] up into the mountain, and sat there. And there came unto him great multitudes, having with them lame, and blind, and dumb, and maimed, and many others, and [3] they cast them at the feet of Jesus: for they had seen all the signs which he did in [4] Jerusalem, when they were gathered at the feast. And he healed them all. And those multitudes marveled when they saw dumb *men* speak, and maimed *men* healed, and lame *men* walk, and blind *men* see; and they praised the God of Israel.

[5] And Jesus called his disciples, and said unto them, I have compassion on this multitude, because of their continuing with me three days, having nothing to eat; and to send them away fasting I am not willing, lest they faint in the way, some of them having [6] [Arabic, p. 89] come from far. His disciples said unto him, Whence have we in the desert [7] bread wherewith to satisfy all this multitude? Jesus said unto them, How [8] many loaves have ye? They said unto him, Seven, and a few small fishes. And he [9] commanded the multitudes to sit down upon the ground; and he took those seven loaves and the fish, and blessed, and brake, and gave to his

disciples to set before [10] them; and the disciples set before the multitudes. And they all ate, and were satisfied: and they took that which remained over of the fragments, seven basketfuls. [11] And the people that ate were four thousand men, besides the women and children. [12] And when the multitudes departed, he went up into the boat, and came to the borders of Magada.

[13] And the Pharisees and Sadducees came to him, and began to seek a discussion with him. And they asked him to shew them a sign from heaven, tempting him. [14] And Jesus sighed within himself, and said, What sign seeks this evil and adulterous generation? It seeks a sign, and it shall not be given a sign, except the sign [15] of Jonah the prophet. Verily I say unto you, This generation shall not be given a [16] sign. And he left them, and went up into the boat, and went away to that side.

[17] And his disciples forgot to take with them bread, and there was not with them [18] in the boat, not even one loaf. And Jesus charged them, and said, Take heed, and guard yourselves from the leaven of the Pharisees and Sadducees, and from the [19] leaven of Herod. And they reflected within themselves that they had taken with them [20] no bread. And Jesus knew, and said unto them, Why think ye within yourselves, O *ye* of little faith, and are anxious, because ye have no bread? Until now do ye not perceive, [21] neither understand? Is your heart yet hard? And have ye eyes, and *yet* see not? [22] [Arabic, p. 90] and have ye ears, and *yet* hear not? And do ye not remember when I brake those five loaves for five thousand? And how many baskets full of broken [23] pieces took ye up? They said, Twelve. He said unto them, And the seven also for four thousand: how many baskets

full of broken pieces took ye up? They [24] said, Seven. He said unto them, How have ye not understood that I spoke not to you because of the bread, but that ye should beware of the leaven of the Pharisees [25] and Sadducees? Then they understood that he spoke, not that they should beware of the leaven of the bread, but of the doctrine of the Pharisees and Sadducees, which he called leaven.

[26] And after that, he came to Bethsaida. And they brought to him a certain blind [27] *man*, and besought him that he would touch him. And he took the hand of that blind man, and led him out without the village, and spat in his eyes, and laid his [28] hand on him, and asked him, What sees thou? And that blind man looked intently, [29] and said unto him, I see men as trees walking. And he placed his hand [30] again on his eyes; and they were restored, and he saw everything clearly. And he sent him to his house, and said, Do not enter even into the village, nor tell any man in the village.

[31] And Jesus went forth, and his disciples, to the villages of Cæsarea Philippi. [32] And while he was going in the way, and his disciples alone, he asked his disciples, [33] and said, What do men say of me that I am, the Son of man? They said unto him, Some say, John the Baptist; and others, Elijah; and others, Jeremiah, or one of the [34, 35] prophets. He said unto them, And ye, what say ye that I am? Simon Cephas answered [36] [Arabic, p. 91] and said, Thou art the Messiah, the Son of the living God. Jesus answered and said unto him, Blessed art thou, Simon son of Jonah: flesh and [37] blood hath not revealed *it* unto thee, but my Father which is in heaven. And I say unto thee also, that thou art Cephas, and on this rock will I build my church; and the [38] gates of Hades

shall not prevail against it. To thee will I give the keys of the kingdom of heaven: and whatsoever thou shalt bind on earth shall be bound in heaven; and [39] whatsoever thou shalt loose on earth shall be loosed in heaven. And he sternly charged his disciples, and warned them that they should not tell any man concerning him, [40] that he was the Messiah. And henceforth began Jesus to shew to his disciples [41] that he was determined to go to Jerusalem, and suffer much, and be rejected of the elders, and of the chief priests, and of the scribes, and be killed, and on the [42] third day rise. And he was speaking plainly. And Simon Cephas, as one grieved [43] for him, said, Far be thou, my Lord, from that. And he turned, and looked upon [44] his disciples, and rebuked Simon, and said, Get thee behind me, Satan: for thou art a stumbling block unto me: for thou thinks not of what pertains to God, but of what pertains to men.

[45] And Jesus called the multitudes with his disciples, and said unto them, Whosoever would come after me, let him deny himself, and take his cross every day, and [46] come after me. And whosoever would save his life shall lose it; and whosoever [47] loses his life for my sake, and for the sake of my gospel, shall save it. What shall [48] a man profit, if he gain all the world, and destroy his own life, or lose it? Or what [49] [Arabic, p. 92] will a man give *in* ransom for his life? Whosoever shall deny me and my sayings in this sinful and adulterous generation, the Son of man also will [50] deny him, when he cometh in the glory of his Father with his holy angels. For the Son of man is about to come in the glory of his Father with his holy angels; and then shall he reward each man according to his works.

Section XXIV.

[1] And he said unto them, Verily I say unto you, There be here now some standing that shall not taste death, until they see the kingdom of God come with strength, and the Son of man who cometh in his kingdom.

[2] And after six days Jesus took Simon Cephas, and James, and John his brother, [3] and brought them up into a high mountain, the three of them only. And while they [4] were praying, Jesus changed, and became after the fashion of another person; and his face shone like the sun, and his raiment was very white like the snow, and as [5] the light of lightning, so that nothing on earth can whiten like it. And there appeared [6] unto him Moses and Elijah talking to Jesus. And they thought that the time [7] of his decease which was to be accomplished at Jerusalem was come. And Simon and those that were with him were heavy in the drowsiness of sleep; and with effort they roused themselves, and saw his glory, and those two men that were standing with him. [8] [Arabic, p. 93] And when they began to depart from him, Simon said unto Jesus, My [9] Master, it is good for us to be here: and if thou wilt, we will make here three tabernacles; one for thee, and one for Moses, and one for Elijah; not knowing [10] what he said, because of the fear which took possession of them. And while he [11] was yet saying that, a bright cloud overshadowed them. And when they saw Moses [12] and Elijah that they had entered into that cloud, they feared again. And a voice was heard out of the cloud, saying, This is my beloved Son, whom I have chosen; [13] hear ye therefore him. And when this voice was heard, Jesus was found alone. [14] And the disciples, when they heard the voice, fell on their faces from the fear which [15] took hold of them.

And Jesus came and touched them and said, Arise, be not [16] afraid. And they lifted up their eyes, and saw Jesus as he was.

[17] And when they went down from the mountain, Jesus charged them, and said unto them, Tell not what ye have seen to any man, until the Son of man rise from [18] among the dead. And they kept the word within themselves, and told no man in [19] those days what they had seen. And they reflected among themselves, What is this [20] word which he spoke unto us, I, when I am risen from among the dead? And his disciples asked him, and said, What is that which the scribes say, then, that Elijah [21] must first come? He said unto them, Elijah cometh first to set in order everything, [Arabic, p. 94] and as it was written of the Son of man, that he should suffer many things, [22] and be rejected. But I say unto you, that Elijah is come, and they knew him not, and have done unto him whatsoever they desired, as it was written of him. [23, 24] In like manner the Son of man is to suffer of them. Then understood the disciples that he spoke unto them concerning John the Baptist.

[25] And on that day whereon they came down from the mountain, there met him a multitude of many people standing with his disciples, and the scribes were discussing [26] with them. And the people, when they saw Jesus, were perplexed, and in the [27] midst of their joy hastened and saluted him. And on that day came certain of the Pharisees, and said unto him, Get thee out, and go hence; for Herod seeks [28] to kill thee. Jesus said unto them, Go ye and say to this fox, Behold, I am casting out demons, and I heal to-day and to-morrow, and on the third day I am perfected. [29] Nevertheless I must be watchful to-day and to-morrow, and on the last day I shall

depart; for it cannot be that a prophet perish outside of Jerusalem.

[30] And after that, there came to him a man from that multitude, and fell upon his knees, and said unto him, I beseech thee, my Lord, look upon my son; he is my [31] only *child*: and the spirit cometh upon him suddenly. A lunacy hath come upon [32] him, and he meets with evils. And when it comes upon him, it beats him about; [33] and he foamed, and gnashed his teeth, and wasted; and many times it hath thrown him into the water and into the fire to destroy him, and it hardly leaves him after [34] [Arabic, p. 95] bruising him. And I brought him near to thy disciples, and they could [35] not heal him. Jesus answered and said, O faithless and perverse generation, till when shall I be with you? And till when shall I bear with you? Bring thy son [36] hither. And he brought him unto him: and when the spirit saw him, immediately [37] it beat him about; and he fell upon the ground, and was raging and foaming. And Jesus asked his father, How long is the time during which he hath been thus? He [38] said unto him, From his youth until now. But, my Lord, help me wherein thou [39] canst, and have mercy upon me. Jesus said unto him, If thou canst believe! All [40] things are possible to him that believeth. And immediately the father of the child [41] cried out, weeping, and said, I believe, my Lord; help my lack of faith. And when Jesus saw the hastening of the people, and their coming at the sound, he rebuked that unclean spirit, and said to it, Thou dumb spirit that speaks not, I command [42] thee, come out of him, and enter not again into him. And that spirit, devil, cried out much, and bruised him, and came out; and that child fell as one dead, and [43] many thought that he had died. But Jesus took

him by his hand, and raised him [44] up, and gave him to his father; and that child was healed from that hour. And the people all marveled at the greatness of God.

[45] And when Jesus entered into the house, his disciples came, and asked him [46] privately, and said unto him, Why were we not able to heal him? Jesus said unto [Arabic, p. 96] them, Because of your unbelief. Verily I say unto you, If ye have faith as a grain of mustard seed, ye shall say to this mountain, Remove hence; [47] and it shall remove; and nothing shall overcome you. But it is impossible to cast out this kind by anything except by fasting and prayer.

[48] And when he went forth thence, they passed through Galilee: and he would not [49] that any man should know it. And he taught his disciples, and said unto them, [50] Keep ye these sayings in your ears and your hearts: for the Son of man is to be delivered into the hands of men, and they shall kill him; and when he is killed, he [51] shall rise on the third day. But they knew not the word which he spoke unto them, for it was concealed from them, that they should not perceive it; and they feared to [52] ask him about this word. And they were exceeding sorrowful.

Section XXV.
[1] And in that day this thought presented itself to his disciples, and they said, which [2] haply should be the great*est* among them. And when they came to Capernaum, and entered into the house, Jesus said unto them, What were ye considering in the [3] way among yourselves? And they were silent because they had considered that *matter*.

[4] And when Simon went forth without, those that received two dirhams for the tribute came to Cephas, and said unto him, Doth your master not give his two [5] dirhams? He said unto them, Yea. And when Cephas entered the house, Jesus anticipated him, and said unto him, What thinks thou, Simon? The kings of the earth, from whom do they receive custom and tribute? From their sons, or from [6] [Arabic, p. 97] strangers? Simon said unto him, From strangers. Jesus said unto him, Children then are free. Simon said unto him, Yea. Jesus said unto him, [7] Give thou also unto them, like the stranger. But, lest it trouble them, go thou to the sea, and cast *a* hook; and the first fish that cometh up, open its mouth, *and* thou shalt find a stater: take therefore that, and give for me and thee.

[8] And in that hour came the disciples to Jesus, and said unto him, Who, thinks [9] thou, is greater in the kingdom of heaven? And Jesus knew the thought of their heart, and called a child, and set him in the midst, and took him in his arms, and [10] said unto them, Verily I say unto you, If ye do not return, and become as children, [11] ye shall not enter the kingdom of heaven. Everyone that shall receive in my name such as this child hath received me: and whosoever receives me receives [12] not me, but him that sent me. And he who is little in your company, the same [13] shall be great. But whosoever shall injure one of these little ones that believe in me, it were better for him that a great millstone should be hanged about his neck, and *he should be* drowned in the depths of the sea.

[14] John answered and said, Our Master, we saw one casting out devils in thy name; [15] and we prevented him, because he followed not thee with us. Jesus said unto

them, Prevent him not; for no man doeth powers in my name, and can hasten to speak evil [16, 17] of me. Everyone who is not in opposition to you is with you. Woe unto the world [Arabic, p. 98] because of trials! But woe unto that man by whose hand the trials come! [18] If thy hand or thy foot injure thee, cut it off, and cast it from thee; for it is better for thee to enter into life being halt or maimed, and not that thou should have two hands or two feet, and fall into the hell of fire that burns forever; [19, 20] where their worm dies not, and their fire is not quenched. And if thine eye seduce [21] thee, pluck it out, and cast it from thee; for it is better for thee to enter the kingdom of God with one eye, than that thou should have two eyes, and fall into the [22, 23] fire of Gehenna; where their worm dies not, and their fire is not quenched. Every [24] *one* shall be salted with fire, and every sacrifice shall be salted with salt. How good [25] is salt! But if the salt also be tasteless, wherewith shall it be salted? It is fit neither for the land nor for dung, but they cast it out. He that hath ears to hear, let him [26] hear. Have ye salt in yourselves, and be in peace one with another.

[27] And he arose from thence, and came to the borders of Judæa beyond Jordan: and there went unto him thither great multitudes, and he healed them; and he taught [28] them also, according to his custom. And the Pharisees came unto him, tempting [29] him, and asking him, Is it lawful for a man to put away his wife? He said, What [30] did Moses command you? They said, Moses made it allowable for us, *saying*, Whosoever [31] will, let him write a writing of divorcement, and put away his wife. Jesus answered and said unto them, Have ye not read, He that made *them* from the beginning [32] made them male and female, and said, For this reason shall the

man leave his father [Arabic, p. 99] and his mother, and cleave to his wife; and they both shall be one body? [33] So then they are not twain, but one body; the thing, then, which God hath [34] joined together, let no man put asunder. And those Pharisees said unto him, Why did Moses consent that a *man* should give a writing of divorcement and put her away? [35] Jesus said unto them, Moses because of the hardness of your hearts gave you leave [36] to divorce your wives; but in the beginning it was not so. I say unto you, Whosoever puts away his wife without fornication, and marries another, hath exposed [37] her to adultery. And his disciples, when he entered the house, asked him again [38] about that. And he said unto them, Everyone who puts away his wife, and [39] marries another, hath exposed her to adultery. And any woman that leaves her husband, and becomes another's, hath committed adultery. And whosoever marries [40] her that is divorced hath committed adultery. And his disciples said unto him, If there be between the man and the woman such a case as this, it is not good for [41] a man to marry. He said unto them, Not every man can endure this saying, except [42] him to whom it is given. There are eunuchs which from their mother's womb were born so; and there are eunuchs which through men became eunuchs; and there are eunuchs which made themselves eunuchs for the sake of the kingdom of heaven. He that is able to be content, let him be content.

[43] Then they brought to him children, that he should lay his hand upon them, and [44] pray: and his disciples were rebuking those that were bringing them. And Jesus saw, and it was distressing to him; and he said unto them, Suffer the children to [Arabic, p. 100] come unto me, and prevent them not; for those that are like

these have [45] the kingdom of God. Verily I say unto you, Whosoever receives not the [46] kingdom of God as this child, shall not enter it. And he took them in his arms, and laid his hand upon them, and blessed them.

Section XXVI.

[1, 2] And there came unto him publicans and sinners to hear his word. And the scribes and the Pharisees murmured, and said, This man receives sinners, and [3] eats with them. And Jesus, when he beheld their murmuring, spoke unto them [4] this parable: What man of you, having an hundred sheep, if one of them were lost, would not leave the ninety-nine in the wilderness, and go and seek the straying *one* [5] till he found it? Verily I say unto you, When he finds it, he will rejoice over it [6] more than *over* the ninety-nine that went not astray; and bear it on his shoulders, and bring it to his house, and call his friends and neighbors, and say unto them, [7] Rejoice with me, since I have found my straying sheep. So your Father which is in heaven wills not that one of these little ones that have strayed should perish, [8] and he seeks for them repentance. I say unto you, Thus there shall be rejoicing in heaven over one sinner that repents, more than *over* ninety-nine righteous persons that do not need repentance.

[9] And what woman having ten drachmas would lose one of them, and not light a [10] lamp, and sweep the house, and seek it with care till she found it; and when she found it, call her friends and neighbors, and say unto them, Rejoice with me, as I [11] have found my drachma that was lost? I say unto you, Thus there shall be joy [Arabic, p. 101] before the angels of God over the one

sinner that repents, more than over the ninety-nine righteous *persons* that do not need repentance.

[12, 13] And Jesus spoke unto them also another parable: A man had two sons: and the younger son said unto him, My father, give me my portion that belonged to [14] me of thy goods. And he divided between them his property. And after a few days the younger son gathered everything that belonged to him, and went into a [15] far country, and there squandered his property by living prodigally. And when he had exhausted everything he had, there occurred a great dearth in that country. [16] And when he was in want, he went and joined himself to one of the people of a city [17] of that country; and that *man* sent him into the field to feed the swine. And he used to long to fill his belly with the carob that those swine were eating: and no man [18] gave him. And when he returned unto himself, he said, How many hired servants now in my father's house have bread enough and to spare, while I here perish with [19] hunger! I will arise and go to my father's house, and say unto him, My father, I [20] have sinned in heaven and before thee, and am not worthy now to be called thy [21] son: make me as one of thy hired servants. And he arose, and came to his father. But his father saw him while he was at a distance, and was moved with compassion [22] for him, and ran, and fell on his breast, and kissed him. And his son said unto him, My father, I have sinned in heaven and before thee, and am not worthy to be [23] called thy son. His father said unto his servants, Bring forth a stately robe, and put [24] *it* on him; and put a ring on his hand, and put on him shoes on his feet: and bring and [25] slay a fatted ox, that we may eat and make merry: for this my son was dead, and is [26] [Arabic, p. 102] alive; and was lost, and is found. And

they began to be merry. Now his elder son was in the field; and when he came and drew near to the house, [27] he heard the sound of many singing. And he called one of the lads, and asked him [28] what this was. He said unto him, Thy brother hath arrived; and thy father hath [29] slain a fatted ox, since he hath received him safe and sound. And he was angry, [30] and would not enter; so his father went out, and besought him to enter. And he said to his father, How many years do I serve thee in bondage, and I never transgressed a commandment of thine; and thou hast never given me a kid, that I might [31] make merry with my friends? But this thy son, when he had squandered thy [32] property with harlots, and come, thou hast slain for him a fatted ox. His father said unto him, My son, thou art at all times with me, and everything I have is [33] thine. It behooved thee to rejoice and make merry, since this thy brother was dead, and is alive; and *was* lost, and is found.

[34] And he spoke a parable unto his disciples: There was a rich man, and he had [35] a steward; and he was accused to him that he had squandered his property. So his lord called him, and said unto him, What is this that I hear regarding thee? Give me the account of thy stewardship; for it is now impossible that thou should [36] be a steward for me. The steward said within himself, What shall I do, seeing that my lord taketh from me the stewardship? To dig I am not able; and to beg I [37] am ashamed. I know what I will do, that, when I go out of the stewardship, they [38] may receive me into their houses. And he called one after another of his lord's [39] debtors, and said to the first, How much owes thou my lord? He said unto him, An hundred portions of oil. He said unto him, Take thy writing, and sit down, and write [40]

quickly fifty portions. And he said to the next, And thou, how much owes thou my lord? He said unto him, An hundred cors of wheat. He said unto him, Take [41] [Arabic, p. 103] thy writing, and sit down, and write eighty cors. And our lord commended the sinful steward because he had done a wise deed; for the children [42] of this world are wiser than the children of the light in this their age. And I also say unto you, Make unto yourselves friends with the wealth of this unrighteousness; [43] so that, when it is exhausted, they may receive you into their tents forever. He who is faithful in a little is faithful also in much: and he who is unrighteous in a [44] little is unrighteous also in much. If then in the wealth of unrighteousness ye were [45] not trustworthy, who will entrust you with the truth? If ye are not found faithful in what does not belong to you, who will give you what belonged to you?

Section XXVII.

[1] Therefore the kingdom of heaven is like a certain king, who would make a [2] reckoning with his servants. And when he began to make *it*, they brought to him one who [3] owed him ten talents. And because he had not wherewith to pay, his lord ordered that he should be sold, he, and his wife, and children, and all that he [4] had, and payment be made. So that servant fell down and worshipped *him*, and said unto him, My lord, have patience with me, and I shall pay thee everything. [5] And the lord of that servant had compassion, and released him, and forgave him his [6] debt. And that servant went out, and found one of his fellow-*servants*, who owed him [Arabic, p. 104] a hundred pence; and he took him, and dealt severely with him, and said [7] unto him, Give me

what thou owes. So the fellow-servant fell down at his [8] feet, and besought him, and said, Grant me respite, and I will pay thee. And he would not; but took him, and cast him into prison, till he should give him his debt. [9] And when their fellow-*servants* saw what happened, it distressed them much; and [10] they came and told their lord of all that had taken place. Then his lord called him, and said unto him, *Thou* wicked servant, all that debt I forgave thee, because [11] thou besought me: was it not then incumbent on thee also to have mercy on thy [12] fellow-servant, as I had mercy on thee? And his lord became wroth, and delivered [13] him to the scourgers, till he should pay all that he owed. So shall my Father which is in heaven do unto you, if one forgive not his brother his wrong conduct from [14] his heart. Take heed within yourselves: if thy brother sin, rebuke him; and if he [15] repent, forgive him. And if he act wrongly towards thee seven times in a day, and on that day return seven times unto thee, and say, I repent towards thee; forgive him. [16] And if thy brother act wrongly towards thee, go and reprove him between thee and [17] him alone: if he hear thee, thou hast gained thy brother. But if he hear thee not, take with thee one or two, and so at the mouth of two or three every saying shall [18] be established. And if he listen not to these also, tell the congregation; and if he listen not even to the congregation, let him be unto thee as a publican and a Gentile. [19] Verily I say unto you, All that ye bind on earth shall be bound in heaven: [20] and what ye loose on earth shall be loosed in heaven. I say unto you also, If two of you agree on earth to ask, everything shall be granted them from my Father [21] [Arabic, p. 105] which is in heaven. For where two or three are gathered in my name, there [22] am I amongst them. Then Cephas drew near to him, and said unto him, My Lord, how many times, if my brother act wrongly towards me, should I forgive him? [23] until seven times? Jesus said unto him, I say not unto thee, Until seven; but, Until seventy [24] times seven, seven. And the servant that knows his lord's will, and makes not [25] ready for him according to his will, shall meet with much punishment; but he that knows not, and doeth something for which he merited punishment, shall meet with slight punishment. Every one to whom much hath been given, much shall be asked of him; and he that hath had much committed to him, much shall be [26] required at his hand. I came to cast fire upon the earth; and I would that it had [27] been kindled already. And I have a baptism to be baptized with, and greatly am [28] I straitened till it be accomplished. See *that ye* despise not one of these little ones that believe in me. Verily I say unto you, Their angels at all times see the [29] face of my Father which is in heaven. The Son of man came to save the thing which was lost.

[30] And after that, Jesus walked in Galilee; and he did not like to walk in Judæa, [31] because the Jews sought to kill him. And there came people who told him of [32] the Galilæans, those whose blood Pilate had mingled with their sacrifices. Jesus answered and said unto them, Do ye imagine that those Galilæans were sinners [33] more than all the Galilæans, so that this thing has come upon them? Nay. Verily I say unto you now, that ye shall all also, if ye repent not, likewise perish. [34] Or perchance those eighteen on whom the palace fell in Siloam, and slew them, do ye imagine that they were to be condemned more than all the people that dwell [35]

[Arabic, p. 106] in Jerusalem? Nay. Verily I say unto you, If ye do not all repent, ye shall perish like them.

[36] And he spoke unto them this parable: A man had a fig tree planted in his vineyard; [37] and he came and sought fruit thereon, and found none. So he said to the husbandman, Lo, three years do I come and seek fruit on this fig tree, and find [38] none: cut it down; why doth it render the ground unoccupied? The husbandman said unto him, My lord, leave it this year also, that I may dig about it, and dung [39] it; then if it bear fruit—! And if not, then cut it down in the coming year.

[40] And when Jesus was teaching on the Sabbath day in one of the synagogues, [41] there was there a woman that had a spirit of disease eighteen years; and she was [42] bowed down, and could not straighten herself at all. And Jesus saw her, and called [43] her, and said unto her, Woman, be loosed from thy disease. And he put his hand [44] upon her; and immediately she was straightened, and praised God. And the chief of the synagogue answered with anger, because Jesus had healed on a Sabbath, and said unto the multitudes, There are six days in which work ought to be done; [45] come in them and be healed, and not on the Sabbath day. But Jesus answered and said unto him, *Ye* hypocrites, doth not each of you on the Sabbath day loose [46] his ox or his ass from the manger, and go and water it? Ought not this woman, who is a daughter of Abraham, and whom the devil hath bound eighteen years, [47] to be loosed from this bond on the Sabbath day? And when he said this, they were all put to shame, those standing, who were opposing him: and all the people were pleased with all the wonders that proceeded from his hand.

Section XXVIII.

[1, 2] [Arabic, p. 107] And at that time the feast of tabernacles of the Jews drew near. So the brethren of Jesus said unto him, Remove now hence, and go to Judæa, that [3] thy disciples may see the deeds that thou does. For no man does a thing secretly [4] and wishes to be apparent. If thou does this, show thyself to the world. For [5] up to this time not even the brethren of Jesus believed on him. Jesus said unto them, My time till now has not arrived; but as for you, your time is always ready. [6] It is not possible for the world to hate you; but me it hated, for I bear witness [7] against it, that its deeds are evil. As for you, go ye up unto this feast: but I go [8] not up now to this feast; for my time has not yet been completed. He said this, and remained behind in Galilee.

[9] 1941But when his brethren went up unto the feast, he journeyed from Galilee, and [10] came to the borders of Judæa, to *the country* beyond Jordan; and there came after [11] him great multitudes, and he healed them all there. And he went out, and proceeded [12] to the feast, not openly, but as one that conceals himself. And the Jews sought him [13] at the feast, and said, In what place is this *man?* And there occurred much murmuring there in the great multitude that came to the feast, on his account. For [14] some said, He is good: and others said, Nay, but he leads the people astray. But no man spoke of him openly for fear of the Jews.

[15] [Arabic, p. 108] But when the days of the feast of tabernacles were half over, Jesus went [16] up to the temple, and taught. And the Jews wondered, and said, How doth [17] this man know writing, seeing he hath not learned? Jesus answered and said, My doctrine [18] is not mine, but his that sent me. Whoever wishes to do his will

understands my doctrine, whether it be from God, or whether I speak of mine own accord. [19] Whosoever speaks of his own accord seeks praise for himself; but whosoever seeks praise for him that sent him, he is true, and unrighteousness in his heart [20] there is none. Did not Moses give you the law, and no man of you kept the [21] law? Why seek to kill me? The multitude answered and said unto him, Thou [22] hast demons: who seeks to kill thee? Jesus answered and said unto them, I did [23] one deed, and ye all marvel because of this. Moses hath given you circumcision (not because it is from Moses, but it is from the fathers); and ye on the Sabbath [24] circumcise a man. And if a man is circumcised on the Sabbath day, that the law of Moses may not be broken; are ye angry at me, because I healed on the Sabbath [25] day the whole man? Judge not with hypocrisy, but judge righteous judgement.

[26] And some people from Jerusalem said, Is not this he whom they seek to slay? [27] And lo, he discourses with them openly, and they say nothing unto him. Think [28] you that our elders have learned that this is the Messiah indeed? But this man is known whence he is; and the Messiah, when he cometh, no man knows whence [29] he is. So Jesus lifted up his voice as he taught in the temple, and said, Ye both know me, and know whence I am; and of my own accord am I not come, but he [30] [Arabic, p. 109] that sent me is true, he whom ye know not: but I know him; for I am [31] from him, and he sent me. And they sought to seize him: and no man [32] laid a hand on him, because his hour had not yet come. But many of the multitude believed on him; and they said, The Messiah, when he cometh, can it be that he will do more than these signs that this *man* doeth?

[33] And a man of that multitude said unto our Lord, Teacher, say to my brother [34] that he divide with me the inheritance. Jesus said unto him, Man, who is it that [35] appointed me over you as a judge and divider? And he said unto his disciples, Take heed within yourselves of all inordinate desire; for it is not in abundance of [36] possessions that life shall be. And he gave them this parable: The ground of a [37] rich man brought forth abundant produce: and he pondered within himself, and [38] said, What shall I do, since I have no place to store my produce? And he said, I will do this: I will pull down the buildings of my barns, and build them, and make [39] them greater; and store there all my wheat and my goods. And I will say to my soul, Soul, thou hast much goods laid by for many years; take thine ease, eat, [40] drink, enjoy thyself. God said unto him, O *thou* of little intelligence, this night shall thy soul be taken from thee; and this that thou hast prepared, whose shall it [41] be? So is he that lays up treasures for himself, and is not rich in God.

[42] And while Jesus was going in the way, there came near to him a young man of the rulers, and fell on his knees, and asked him, and said, Good Teacher, what is [43] it that I must do that I may have eternal life? Jesus said unto him, Why calls thou [44] me good, while there is none good but the one, *even* God? Thou knows the commandments. [45] If thou would enter into life, keep the commandments. The young [Arabic, p. 110] man said unto him, Which of the commandments? Jesus said unto him, [46] Thou shalt not commit adultery, Thou shalt not steal, Thou shalt not kill, Thou shalt not bear false witness, Thou shalt not do injury, Honor thy father [47] and thy mother: and, Love thy neighbor as thyself. That

young man said unto [48] him, All these have I kept from my youth: what then is it that I lack? And Jesus [49] looked intently at him, and loved him, and said unto him, If thou would be perfect, what thou lacks is one thing: go away and sell everything that thou hast, and give to the poor, and thou shalt have treasure in heaven: and take thy [50] cross, and follow me. And that young man frowned at this word, and went away [51] feeling sad; for he was very rich. And when Jesus saw his sadness, he looked towards his disciples, and said unto them, How hard it is for them that have possessions to enter the kingdom of God!

Section XXIX.

[1] Verily I say unto you, It is difficult for a rich man to enter the kingdom of [2] heaven. And I say unto you also, that it is easier for a camel to enter the eye of [3] a needle, than for a rich man to enter the kingdom of God. And the disciples were wondering at these sayings. And Jesus answered and said unto them again, My children, how hard it is for those that rely on their possessions to enter the [4] kingdom of God! And those that were listening wondered more, and said amongst [5] themselves, being agitated, Who, thinks thou, can be saved? And Jesus looked at them intently, and said unto them, With men this is not possible, but with God *it is:* [6] [Arabic, p. 111] it is possible for God to do everything. Simon Cephas said unto him, Lo, we have left everything, and followed thee; what is it, thinks thou, that we [7] shall have? Jesus said unto them, Verily I say unto you, Ye that have followed me, in the new world, when the Son of

man shall sit on the throne of his glory, ye also [8] shall sit on twelve thrones, and shall judge the twelve tribes of Israel. Verily I say unto you, No man leaves houses, or brothers, or sisters, or father, or mother, or wife, or children, or kinsfolk, or lands, because of the kingdom of God, or for [9] my sake, and the sake of my gospel, who shall not obtain many times as much in this [10] time, and in the world to come inherit eternal life: and now in this time, houses, and brothers, and sisters, and mothers, and children, and lands, with persecution; [11] and in the world to come *ever*lasting life. Many that are first shall be last, and that are last shall be first.

[12] And when the Pharisees heard all this, because of their love for wealth they [13] scoffed at him. And Jesus knew what was in their hearts, and said unto them, Ye are they that justify yourselves before men; while God knows your hearts: the thing that is lofty with men is base before God.

[14] And he began to say, A *certain* man was rich, and wore silk and purple, and enjoyed [15] himself every day in splendor: and there was a poor man named Lazarus, and [16] he was cast down at the door of the rich man, afflicted with sores, and he longed to fill [Arabic, p. 112] his belly with the crumbs that fell from the table of that rich man; yea, [17] even the dogs used to come and lick his sores. And it happened that that poor man died, and the angels conveyed him into the bosom of Abraham: and the [18] rich man also died, and was buried. And while he was being tormented in Hades, [19] he lifted up his eyes from afar, and saw Abraham with Lazarus in his bosom. And he called with a loud voice, and said, My father Abraham, have mercy upon me, and send Lazarus to wet the tip of his finger with water, and moisten my

tongue [20] for me; for, behold, I am burned in this flame. Abraham said unto him, My son, remember that thou received the good things in thy life, and Lazarus his afflictions: [21] but now, behold, he is at rest here, and thou art tormented. And in addition to all this, there is between us and you a great abyss placed, so that they that would cross unto you from hence cannot, nor yet from thence do they cross unto [22] us. He said unto him, Then I beseech thee, my father, to send him to my father's [23] house; for I have five brethren; let him go, that they also sin not, and come to [24] the abode of this torment. Abraham said unto him, They have Moses and the [25] prophets; let them hear them. He said unto him, Nay, my father Abraham: but [26] let a man from the dead go unto them, and they will repent. Abraham said unto him, If they listen neither to Moses nor to the prophets, neither if a man from the dead rose would they believe him.

[27] The kingdom of heaven is like a man that is a householder, which went out early [28] in the morning to hire laborers for his vineyard. And he agreed with the laborers on [29] one penny a day for each laborer, and he sent them into his vineyard. And he went [30] [Arabic, p. 113] out in three hours, and saw others standing in the market idle. He said unto them, Go ye also into my vineyard, and what is right I will pay you. [31] And they went. And he went out also at the sixth and the ninth hour, and did likewise, [32] and sent them. And about the eleventh hour he went out, and found others standing idle. He said unto them, Why are ye standing the whole day idle? [33] They said unto him, Because no one hath hired us. He said unto them, Go ye [34] also into the vineyard, and what is right ye shall receive. So when evening came, the lord of the vineyard said unto his steward, Call the

laborers, and pay them [35] their wages; and begin with the later ones, and end with the former ones. And [36] those of eleven hours came, and received each a penny. When therefore the first came, they supposed that they should receive something more; and they also [37] received each a penny. And when they received *it*, they spoke angrily against the [38] householder, and said, These last worked one hour, and thou hast made them equal [39] with us, who have suffered the heat of the day, and its burden. He answered and said unto one of them, My friend, I do thee no wrong: *was it* not for a penny *that* [40] thou didst bargain with me? Take what is thine, and go thy way; for I wish to [41] give this last as I have given thee. Or am I not entitled to do with what is mine [42] what I choose? Or is thine eye perchance evil, because I am good? Thus shall the last *ones* be first, and the first last. The called are many, and the chosen are few.

[43] And when Jesus entered into the house of one of the chiefs of the Pharisees to eat bread on the Sabbath day, and they were watching him to see what he would [44, 45] do, and there was before him a man which had the dropsy, Jesus answered and [46] said unto the scribes and the Pharisees, Is it lawful on the Sabbath to heal? But [Arabic, p. 114] they were silent. So he took him, and healed him, and sent him away. [47] And he said unto them, Which of you shall *have* his son or his ox fall on the Sabbath day into a well, and not lift him up straightway, and draw water for [48] him? And they were not able to answer him a word to that.

Section XXX.

[1] And he spoke a parable unto those which were bidden there, because he saw [2] them choose the places

that were in the highest part of the sitting room: When a man invites thee to a feast, do not go and sit at the head of the room; lest there [3] be there a man more honorable than thou, and he that invited you come and say unto thee, Give the place to this man: and thou be ashamed when thou rises and [4] takes another place. But when thou art invited, go and sit last; so that when he that invited thee cometh, he may say unto thee, My friend, go up higher: and [5] thou shalt have praise before all that were invited with thee. For every one that exalted himself shall be abased; and every one that abased himself shall be exalted.

[6] And he said also to him that had invited him, When thou makes a feast or a banquet, do not invite thy friends, nor even thy brethren, nor thy kinsmen, nor thy [7] rich neighbors; lest haply they also invite thee, and thou have this reward. But when thou makes a feast, invite the poor, and those with withered hand, and the [8] lame, and the blind: and blessed art thou, since they have not the means to reward [9] thee; that thy reward may be at the rising of the righteous. And when one of them that were invited heard that, he said unto him, Blessed is he that shall eat bread in the kingdom of God.

[10, 11] Jesus answered again in parables, and said, The kingdom of heaven hath been likened [Arabic, p. 115] to a certain king, which made a feast for his son, and prepared a [12] great banquet, and invited many: and he sent his servants at the time of the feast to inform them that were invited, Everything is made ready for you; come. And [13] they would not come, but began all of them with one voice to make excuse. And the first said unto them, Say to him, I have bought a field, and I must needs go out [14] to see it: I pray thee to release me, for I

ask to be excused. And another said, I have bought five yoke of oxen, and I am going to examine them: I pray thee [15] to release me, for I ask to be excused. And another said, I have married a wife, [16] and therefore I cannot come. And the king sent also other servants, and said, Say to those that were invited, that my feast is ready, and my oxen and my fatlings are [17] slain, and everything is ready: come to the feast. But they made light of it, and [18] went, one to his field, and another to his merchandise: 2078and the rest took his [19] servants, and entreated them shamefully, and killed them. And one of the servants [20] came, and informed his lord of what had happened. And when the king heard, he became angry, and sent his armies; and they destroyed those murderers, and [21] burned their cities. Then he said to his servants, The feast is prepared, but those [22] that were invited were not worthy. Go out quickly into the markets and into the partings of the ways of the city, and bring in hither the poor, and those with pains, and the lame, and the blind. And the servants did as the king commanded them. [23] And they came, and said unto him, Our lord, we have done all that thou commanded [24] us, and there is here still room. So the lord said unto his servants, Go out into the roads, and the ways, and the paths, and every one that ye find, invite [25] [Arabic, p. 116] to the feast, and constrain them to enter, till my house is filled. I say unto you, that no one of those people that were invited shall taste of my feast. [26] And those servants went out into the roads, and gathered all that they found, good and [27] bad: and the banquet-house was filled with guests. And the king entered to see those [28] who were seated, and he saw there a man not wearing a festive garment: and he said unto him, My friend, how didst thou come in here not having on festive garments? [29] And he was silent. Then the king said to the servants, Bind his hands and his feet, and put him forth into the outer darkness; there shall be weeping and [30] gnashing of teeth. The called are many; and the chosen, few.

[31] And after that, the time of the feast of unleavened bread of the Jews arrived, [32] and Jesus went out to go to Jerusalem. And as he went in the way, there met him [33] ten persons who were lepers, and stood afar off: and they lifted up their voice, and [34] said, Our Master, Jesus, have mercy upon us. And when he saw them, he said unto them, Go and shew yourselves unto the priests. And when they went, they [35] were cleansed. And one of them, when he saw himself cleansed, returned, and [36] was praising God with a loud voice; and he fell on his face before the feet of [37] Jesus, giving him thanks: and this *man* was a Samaritan. Jesus answered and said, [38] Were not those that were cleansed ten? Where then are the nine? Not one of them turned aside to come and praise God, but this *man* who is of a strange [39] people. He said unto him, Arise, and go thy way; for thy faith hath given thee life.

[40] And while they were going up in the way to Jerusalem, Jesus went in front of them; and they wondered, and followed him fearing. And he took his twelve disciples apart, [41] and began to tell them privately what was about to befall him. And he said unto [Arabic, p. 117] them, We are going up to Jerusalem, and all the things shall be fulfilled [42] that are written in the prophets concerning the Son of man. He shall be delivered to the chief priests and the scribes; and they shall condemn him to death, [43] and deliver him to the peoples; and they shall treat him shamefully, and scourge

[44] him, and spit in his face, and humble him, and crucify him, and slay him: and on [45] the third day he shall rise. But they understood not one thing of this; but this word was hidden from them, and they did not perceive these things that were addressed to them.

[46] Then came near to him the mother of the (two) sons of Zebedee, she and her (two) sons, and worshipped him, and asked of him a *certain* thing. And he said [47] unto her, What would thou? And James and John, her two sons, came forward, and said unto him, Teacher, we would that all that we ask thou would [48] do unto us. He said unto them, What would ye that I should do unto you? [49] They said unto him, Grant us that we may sit, the one on thy right, and the other [50] on thy left, in thy kingdom and thy glory. And Jesus said unto them, Ye know not what ye ask. Are ye able to drink the cup that I am to drink? And with the [51] baptism that I am to be baptized with, will ye be baptized? And they said unto him, We are able. Jesus said unto them, The cup that I drink ye shall drink; and [52] with the baptism wherewith I am baptized ye shall be baptized: but that ye should sit on my right and on my left is not mine to give; but *it is* for him for whom my Father hath prepared *it*.

Section XXXI.
[1] And when the ten heard, they were moved with anger against James and John. [2] And Jesus called them, and said unto them, Ye know that the rulers of the nations [3] are their lords; and their great men are set in authority over them. Not thus shall it [Arabic, p. 118] be amongst you: but he amongst you that would be great, let him be to you a [4] servant; and whoever of you would be first, let

him be to every man a [5] bondservant: *even* as the Son of man also came not to be served, but to serve, and [6] to give himself a ransom in place of the many. He said this, and was going about [7] the villages and the cities, and teaching; and he went to Jerusalem. And a man asked him, Are those that shall be saved few? Jesus answered and said unto [8] them, Strive ye to enter at the narrow door: I say unto you now, that many shall [9] seek to enter, and shall not be able from the time when the master of the house rises, and closes the door, and ye shall be standing without, and shall knock at the door, and shall begin to say, Our lord, open unto us; and he shall answer and [10] say, I say unto you, I know you not whence ye are: and ye shall begin to say, [11] Before thee we did eat and drink, and in our markets didst thou teach; and he shall say unto you, I know you not whence ye are; depart from me, ye servants [12] of untruth. There shall be weeping and gnashing of teeth, when ye see Abraham, and Isaac, and Jacob, and all the prophets, in the kingdom of God, while ye are [13] put forth without. And they shall come from the east and the west, and from the [14] north and the south, and shall sit down in the kingdom of God. And there shall then be last that have become first, and first that have become last.

[15, 16] And when Jesus entered and passed through Jericho, there was a man named Zacchæus, [17] rich, and chief of the publicans. And he desired to see Jesus who he was; and he was not able for the pressure of the crowd, because Zacchæus was little of stature. [18] [Arabic, p. 119] And he hastened, and went before Jesus, and went up into an unripe fig [19] tree to see Jesus: for he was to pass thus. And when Jesus came to that place, he saw him, and said unto him, Make haste, and come

down, Zacchæus: [20] today I must be in thy house. And he hastened, and came down, and received [21] him joyfully. And when they all saw, they murmured, and said, He hath gone in [22] and lodged with a man that is a sinner. So Zacchæus stood, and said unto Jesus, My Lord, now half of my possessions I give to the poor, and what I have unjustly [23] taken from every man I give him fourfold. Jesus said unto him, Today is salvation [24] come to this house, because this *man* also is a son of Abraham. For the Son of man came to seek and save the thing that was lost.

[25] And when Jesus went out of Jericho, he and his disciples, there came after him [26] a great multitude. And there was a blind man sitting by the way side begging. [27] And his name was Timæus, the son of Timæus. And he heard the sound of the [28] multitude passing, and asked, Who is this? They said unto him, Jesus the Nazarene [29] passes by. And when he heard that it was Jesus, he called out with a loud [30] voice, and said, Jesus, son of David, have mercy on me. And those that went before Jesus were rebuking him, that he should hold his peace: but he cried the [31] more, and said, Son of David, have mercy on me. And Jesus stood, and commanded that they should call him. And they called the blind man, and said unto [32] him, Be of good courage, and rise; for, behold, he called thee. And the blind [33] man threw away his garment, and rose, and came to Jesus. Jesus said unto him, What dost thou wish that I should do unto thee? And that blind man said unto him, My Lord and Master, that my eyes may be opened, so that I may see thee. [34] [Arabic, p. 120] And Jesus had compassion on him, and touched his eyes, and said unto [35] him, See; for thy faith hath saved thee. And immediately he

received his sight, and came after him, and praised God; and all the people that saw praised God.

[36] And he spoke a parable because he was nearing Jerusalem, and they supposed [37] that at that time the kingdom of God was about to appear. He said unto them, A man, a son of a great race, went into a far country, to receive a kingdom, and [38] return. And he called his ten servants, and gave them ten shares, and said unto [39] them, Trade till the time of my coming. But the people of his city hated him, and [40] sent messengers after him, and said, We will not that this *man* reign over us. And when he had received a kingdom, and returned, he said that the servants to whom he had given the money should be called unto him, that he might know what each [41] of them had traded. And the first came, and said, My lord, thy share hath gained [42] ten shares. The king said unto him, Thou good and faithful servant, who hast [43] been found faithful in a little, be thou set over ten districts. And the second came, [44] and said, My lord, thy portion hath gained five portions. And he said unto him [45] also, And thou shalt be set over five districts. And another came, and said, My [46] lord, here is thy portion, which was with me laid by in a napkin: I feared thee, because thou art a hard man, and takes what thou did not leave, and seeks [47] what thou did not give, and reaps what thou didst not sow. His lord said unto him, From thy mouth shall I judge thee, thou wicked and idle servant, who was untrustworthy. Thou knew that I am a hard man, and take what I did not [48] leave, and reap what I did not sow: why didst thou not put my money at usury, [49] and so I might come and seek it, with its gains? And he said unto those that were standing in front of him, Take from him the share, and give it to him that

hath [50, 51] [Arabic, p. 121] ten shares. They said unto him, Our lord, he hath ten shares. He said unto them, I say unto you, Everyone that hath shall be given unto; and [52] he that hath not, that which he hath also shall be taken from him. And those mine enemies who would not that I should reign over them, bring them, and slay them before me.

Section XXXII.

[1] And when Jesus entered Jerusalem, he went up to the temple of God, and found [2] there oxen and sheep and doves. And when he beheld those that sold and those that bought, and the money-changers sitting, he made for himself a scourge of rope, and drove them all out of the temple, and the sheep and the oxen, and the money-changers; and he threw down their money, and upset their tables, and the seats of [3] them that sold the doves; and he was teaching, and saying unto them, Is it not written, My house is a house of prayer for all peoples? And ye have made it a den [4] for robbers. And he said unto those that sold the doves, Take this hence, and [5] make not my Father's house a house of merchandise. And he suffered not any [6] one to carry vessels inside the temple. And his disciples remembered the scripture, [7] The zeal of thy house hath eaten me up. The Jews answered and said unto him, [8] What sign hast thou shewn us, that thou does this? Jesus answered and said unto [9] them, Destroy this temple, and I shall raise it in three days. The Jews said unto him, This temple was built in forty-six years, and wilt thou raise it in three days? [10] But he spoke unto them of the temple of his body, that when they destroyed it, he [11] [Arabic, p. 122] would raise it in three days. When therefore he rose from among the dead, his

disciples remembered that he said this; and they believed the scriptures, and the word that Jesus spoke.

[12] And when Jesus sat down over against the treasury, he observed how the multitudes were casting their offerings into the treasury: and many rich *men* were [13, 14] throwing in much. And there came a poor widow, and cast in two mites. And Jesus called his disciples, and said unto them, Verily I say unto you, This poor [15] widow cast into the treasury more than all the people: and all of these cast into the place of the offering of God of the superfluity of their wealth; while this *woman* of her want threw in all that she possessed.

[16] And he spoke unto them this parable, concerning people who trusted in themselves [17] that they are righteous, and despised every man: Two men went up to the [18] temple to pray; one of them a Pharisee, and the other a publican. And the Pharisee stood apart, and prayed thus, O Lord, I thank thee, since I am not like the rest of men, the unjust, the profligate, the extortionist, or even like this publican; [19] but I fast two days a week, and tithe all my possessions. And the publican was [20] standing at a distance, and he would not even lift up his eyes to heaven, but was [21] beating upon his breast, and saying, O Lord, have mercy on me, me the sinner. I say unto you, that this man went down justified to his house more than the Pharisee. Everyone that exalted himself shall be abased; and every one that abased himself shall be exalted.

[22] [Arabic, p. 123] And when eventide was come, he left all the people, and went outside the [23] city to Bethany, he and his twelve, and he remained there. And all the people, because they knew the place, came to him, and he received them; and them that [24] had need of

healing he healed. And on the morning of the next day, when he returned [25] to the city from Bethany, he hungered. And he saw a fig tree at a distance on the beaten highway, having on it leaves. And he came unto it, *expecting* to find something on it; and when he came, he found nothing on it but the leaves—it was not [26] the season of figs—and he said unto it, Henceforward for ever let no man eat fruit of thee. And his disciples heard.

[27] And they came to Jerusalem. And there was there a man of the Pharisees, [28] named Nicodemus, ruler of the Jews. This *man* came unto Jesus by night, and said unto him, My Master, we know that thou hast been sent from God as a teacher; and no man can do these signs that thou does, except him whom God is [29] with. Jesus answered and said unto him, Verily, verily, I say unto thee, If a man [30] be not born a second *time*, he cannot see the kingdom of God. Nicodemus said unto him, How can a man who is old be born? Can he, think you, return again to [31] his mother's womb a second time, to enter and be born? Jesus answered and said unto him, Verily, verily, I say unto thee, If a man be not born of water and the Spirit, [32] he cannot enter the kingdom of God. For he that is born of flesh is flesh; and he that [33] is born of Spirit is spirit. Wonder not that I said unto thee that ye must be born a [34] [Arabic, p. 124] second *time*. The wind blows where it listed, and thou hears its voice, but thou knows not from what place it cometh, nor whither it goes: so [35] is every man that is born of the Spirit. Nicodemus answered and said unto him, [36] How can that be? Jesus answered and said unto him, Art thou teaching Israel, [37] and *yet* knows not these things? Verily, verily, I say unto thee, What we know [38] we say, and what we have seen we witness: and ye receive

not our witness. If I said unto you what is on earth, and ye believed not, how then, if I say unto you [39] what is in heaven, will ye believe? And no man hath ascended up into heaven, except him that descended from heaven, the Son of man, which is in heaven. [40] And as Moses lifted up the serpent in the wilderness, so is the Son of man to be [41] lifted up; so that every man who may believe in him may not perish, but have [42] eternal life. God so loved the world, that he should give his only Son; and so everyone that believeth on him should not perish, but should have eternal life. [43] God sent not his Son into the world to judge the world; but that the world might [44] be saved by his hand. He that believeth in him shall not be judged: but he that believeth not is condemned beforehand, because he hath not believed in the name [45] of the only *Son*, the Son of God. This is the judgement, that the light came into the world, and men loved the darkness more than the light; because their deeds [46] were evil. Whosoever doeth evil deeds hated the light, and cometh not to the [47] light, lest his deeds be reproved. But he that doeth the truth cometh to the light, that his deeds may be known, that they have been done in God.

Section XXXIII.

[1] [Arabic, p. 125] And when evening came, Jesus went forth outside of the city, he and his [2] disciples. And as they passed in the morning, the disciples saw that fig tree [3] withered away from its root. And they passed by, and said, How did the fig tree dry [4] up immediately? And Simon remembered, and said unto him, My Master, behold, [5] that fig tree which thou didst curse hath dried up. And Jesus answered and said [6] unto

them, Let there be in you the faith of God. Verily I say unto you, if ye believe, and doubt not in your hearts, and assure yourselves that that will be which [7] ye say, ye shall have what ye say. And if ye say to this mountain, Remove, and [8] fall into the sea, it shall be. And all that ye ask God in prayer, and believe, he [9, 10] will give you. And the apostles said unto our Lord, Increase our faith. He said unto them, If there be in you faith like a grain of mustard, ye shall say to this fig tree, Be thou torn up, and be thou planted in the sea; and it will obey you. [11] Who of you hath a servant driving a yoke of oxen or tending sheep, and if he [12] come from the field, will say unto him straightway, Go and sit down? Nay, he will say unto him, Make ready for me wherewith I may sup, and gird thy waist, and serve me, till I eat and drink; and afterwards thou shalt eat and drink also. [13] Doth that servant haply, who did what he was bid, receive his praise? I think [14] not. So ye also, when ye have done all that ye were bid, say, We are idle servants; what it was our duty to do, we have done.

[15] For this reason I say unto you, Whatever ye pray and ask, believe that ye [16] [Arabic, p. 126] receive, and ye shall have. And when ye stand to pray, forgive what is in your heart against *any* man; and your Father which is in heaven will [17] forgive you also your wrong-doings. But if ye forgive not men their wrong-doings, neither will your Father forgive you also your wrong-doings.

[18] And he spoke unto them a parable also, that they should pray at all times, and [19] not be slothful: There was a judge in a city, who feared not God, nor was ashamed [20] for men: and there was a widow in that city; and she came unto him, and said, [21] Avenge me of mine

adversary. And he would not for a long time: but afterwards he said within himself, If of God I have no fear, and before men I have no shame; [22] *yet* because this widow vexes *me*, I will avenge her, that she come not at all times [23, 24] and annoy me. And our Lord said, Hear ye what the judge of injustice said. And shall not God *still* more do vengeance for his elect, who call upon him in the night [25] and *in* the day, and grant them respite? I say unto you, He will do vengeance for them speedily. Thinks thou the Son of man will come and find faith on the earth?

[26, 27] And they came again to Jerusalem. And it came to pass, on one of the days, as Jesus was walking in the temple, and teaching the people, and preaching *the* [28] *gospel*, that the chief priests and the scribes with the elders came upon him, and said unto him, Tell us: By what power does thou this? And who gave thee this [29] power to do that? And Jesus said unto them, I also will ask you one word, and if [30] ye tell me, I also shall tell you by what power I do that. The baptism of John, from [31] what place *is* it? From heaven or of men? Tell me. And they reflected within themselves, [Arabic, p. 127] and said, If we shall say unto him, From heaven; he will say unto [32] us, For what reason did ye not believe him? But if we shall say, Of men; [33] we fear that the people will stone us, all of them. And all of them were holding [34] to John, that he was a true prophet. They answered and said unto him, We know [35] not. Jesus said unto them, Neither tell I you also by what power I work. What think ye? A man had two sons; and he went to the first, and said unto him, My [36] son, go to-day, and till in the vineyard. And he answered and said, I do not wish [37] to: but finally he repented, and went. And he went to the

other, and said unto [38] him likewise. And he answered and said, Yea, my lord: and went not. Which of these two did the will of his father? They said unto him, The first. Jesus said unto them, Verily I say unto you, The publicans and harlots go before you into [39] the kingdom of God. John came unto you in the way of righteousness, and ye believed him not; but the publicans and harlots believed him; and ye, not even when ye saw, did ye repent at last, that ye might believe in him.

[40] Hear another parable: A man was a householder, and planted a vineyard, and surrounded it with a hedge, and digged in it a winepress, and built in it a tower, [41, 42] and gave it to husbandmen, and went to a distance for a long time. So when the time of the fruits came, he sent his servants unto the husbandmen, that they might [43] send him of the produce of his vineyard. And those husbandmen beat him, and [44] sent him away empty. And he sent unto them another servant also; and they [45] stoned him, and wounded him, and sent him away with shameful handling. And he sent again another; and they slew him. And he sent many other servants unto [46] them. And the husbandmen took his servants, and one they beat, and another they [47] stoned, and another they slew. So he sent again other servants more than the first; and [48] [Arabic, p. 128] they did likewise with them. So the owner of the vineyard said, What shall I do? I will send my beloved son: it may be they will see him and be [49, 50] ashamed. So at last he sent unto them his beloved son that he had. But the husbandmen, when they saw the son, said amongst themselves, This is the heir. [51, 52] And they said, We will slay him, and so the inheritance will be ours. So they took [53] him, and put him forth without the vineyard, and slew him. When then

the lord [54] of the vineyard shall come, what will he do with those husbandmen? They said unto him, He will destroy them in the worst of ways, and give the vineyard to [55] other husbandmen, who will give him fruit in its season. Jesus said unto them, Have ye never read in the scripture,

> The stone which the builders declared to be base,
> The same came to be at the head of the corner:
> [56] From God was this,
> And it is wonderful in our eyes?

[57] Therefore I say unto you, The kingdom of God shall be taken from you, and [58] given to a people that will produce fruit. And whosoever falls on this stone shall be broken in pieces: but on whomsoever it falls, it will grind him to [59] powder. And when the chief priests and the Pharisees heard his parables, they [60] perceived that it was concerning them he spoke. And they sought to seize him; and they feared the multitude, because they were holding to him as the prophet.

Section XXXIV.

[1] Then went the Pharisees and considered how they might ensnare him in a word, [2] and deliver him into the power of the judge, and into the power of the ruler. And they sent unto him their disciples, with the kinsfolk of Herod; and they said unto him, [Arabic, p. 129] Teacher, we know that thou speaks the truth, and teaches the way of God with equity, and art not lifted up by any man: for thou acts not so as to [3] be seen of any man. Tell us now, What is thy opinion? Is it lawful that we should [4] pay the tribute to Cæsar, or not? Shall we give, or shall we not give? But Jesus knew [5] their deceit, and said unto them, Why tempt ye me, ye

hypocrites? Shew me the [6] penny of the tribute. So they brought unto him a penny. Jesus said unto them, To whom belonged this image and inscription? They said unto him, To Cæsar. [7, 8] He said unto them, Give what is Cæsar's to Cæsar, and what is God's to God. And they could not make him slip in a *single* word before the people; and they marveled at his word, and refrained.

[9] And on that day came the Sadducees, and said unto him, There is no life for [10] the dead. And they asked him, and said unto him, Teacher, Moses said unto us, If a man die, not having children, let his brother take his wife, and raise up seed [11] for his brother. Now there *were* with us seven brethren: and the first took a wife, [12] and died without children; and the second took his wife, and died without children; [13] and the third also took her; and in like manner the seven of them also, and they [14, 15] died without leaving children. And last of them all the woman died also. At the resurrection, then, which of these seven shall have this woman? For all of them took [16] her. Jesus answered and said unto them, Is it not for this that ye have erred, [17] because ye know not the scriptures, nor the power of God? And the sons of this [18] world take wives, and the women become the men's; but those that have become worthy of that world, and the resurrection from among the dead, do not take [19] [Arabic, p. 130] wives, and the women also do not become the men's. Nor is it possible that they should die; but they are like the angels, and are the children of [20] God, because they have become the children of the resurrection. For in the resurrection of the dead, have ye not read in the book of Moses, how from the bush God said unto him, I am the God of Abraham, and the God of Isaac, and the God of Jacob? [21] And God is not *the God*

of the dead, but of the living: for all of them are alive with him. And ye have erred greatly.

[22, 23] And when the multitudes heard, they were wondering at his teaching. And [24] some of the scribes answered and said unto him, Teacher, thou hast well said. But the rest of the Pharisees, when they saw his silencing the Sadducees on this point, gathered against him to contend with him.

[25] And one of the scribes, of those that knew the law, when he saw the excellence [26] of his answer to them, desired to try him, and said unto him, What shall I do to inherit eternal life? And, Which of the commandments is greater, and has precedence [27] in the law? Jesus said unto him, The first of all the commandments is, Hear, O [28] Israel; The Lord our God, the Lord is one: and thou shalt love the Lord thy God with all thy heart, and with all thy soul, and with all thy thought, and with all thy [29, 30] strength. This is the great and preeminent commandment. And the second, which is like it, is, Thou shalt love thy neighbor as thyself. And another commandment [31] greater than these two there is not. On these two commandments, then, are hung the [32] [Arabic, p. 131] law and the prophets. That scribe said unto him, Excellent! my Master; thou hast said truly that he is one, and there is no other outside of him: [33] and that a man should love him with all his heart, and with all his thought, and with all his soul, and with all his strength, and that he should love his neighbor as [34] himself, is better than all savors and sacrifices. And Jesus saw him that he had answered wisely; and he answered and said unto him, Thou art not far from the [35, 36] kingdom of God. Thou hast spoken rightly: do this, and thou shalt live. And he, as his desire was to

justify himself, said unto him, And who is my neighbor? [37] Jesus said unto him, A man went down from Jerusalem to Jericho; and the robbers fell upon him, and stripped him, and beat him, his life remaining in him *but* little, [38] and went away. And it happened that there came down a certain priest that way; [39] and he saw him, and passed by. And likewise a Levite also came and reached [40] that place, and saw him, and passed by. And a certain Samaritan, as he journeyed, [41] came to the place where he was, and saw him, and had compassion on him, and came near, and bound up his strokes, and poured on them wine and oil; and he set him on the ass, and brought him to the inn, and expended his care upon him. [42] And on the morrow of that day he took out two pence, and gave them to the innkeeper, and said unto him, Care for him; and if thou spends upon him more, [43] when I return, I shall give thee. Who of these three now, thinks thou, is nearest [44] to him that fell among the robbers? And he said unto him, He that had compassion [45] [Arabic, p. 132] on him. Jesus said unto him, Go, and do thou also likewise. And no man dared afterwards to ask him anything.

[46] And he was teaching every day in the temple. But the chief priests and scribes and the elders of the people sought to destroy him: and they could not *find* what [47] they should do with him; and all the people were hanging upon him to hear him. [48] And many of the multitude believed on him, and said, The Messiah, when he [49] cometh, can it be that he will do more than these signs that this *man* doeth? And the Pharisees heard the multitudes say that of him; and the chief priests sent [50] officers to seize him. And Jesus said unto them, I am with you *but* a short time [51] yet, and I go to him that

sent me. And ye shall seek me, and shall not find me: [52] and where I shall be, ye shall not be able to come. The Jews said within themselves, Whither hath this *man* determined to go that we shall not be able *to find* him? can it be that he is determined to go to the regions of the nations, and teach [53] the heathen? What is this word that he said, Ye shall seek me, and shall not find me: and where I am, ye cannot come?

Section XXXV.

[1] And on the great day, which is the last of the feast, Jesus stood, crying out and [2] saying, If *any* man is thirsty, let him come unto me, and drink. Everyone that believeth in me, as the scriptures said, there shall flow from his belly rivers of pure [3] water. He said that referring to the Spirit, which those who believed in him were to receive: for the Spirit was not yet granted; and because Jesus had not yet been [4] [Arabic, p. 133] glorified. And many of the multitude that heard his words said, This is [5] in truth the prophet. And others said, This is the Messiah. But others [6] said, Can it be that the Messiah will come from Galilee? Hath not the scripture said that from the seed of David, and from Bethlehem, the village of David, the [7] Messiah cometh? And there occurred a dissension in the multitude because of him. [8] And some of them were wishing to seize him; but no man laid a hand upon him.

[9] And those officers came to the chief priests and Pharisees: and the priests said [10] unto them, Why did ye not bring him? The officers said, Never spoke man thus [11] as speaks this man. The Pharisees said unto them, Perhaps ye also have gone [12, 13] astray? Hath any of the rulers or the Pharisees haply believed in him?

Except [14] this people which knows not the law; they are accursed. Nicodemus, one of them, [15] he that had come to Jesus by night, said unto them, Doth our law haply condemn [16] a man, except it hear him first and know what he hath done? They answered and said unto him, Art thou also haply from Galilee? Search, and see that a prophet rises not from Galilee.

[17, 18] And when the Pharisees assembled, Jesus asked them, and said, What say ye of [19] the Messiah? Whose son is he? They said unto him, The son of David. He said unto them, And how doth David in the Holy Spirit call him Lord? For he said,

[20] The Lord said unto my Lord,
Sit on my right hand,
That I may put thine enemies under thy feet.

[21, 22] If then David called him Lord, how is he his son? And no one was able to answer him; and no man dared from that day again to ask him of anything.

[23] And Jesus addressed them again, and said, I am the light of the world; and he that [24] follows me shall not walk in darkness, but shall find the light of life. The Pharisees [Arabic, p. 134] said unto him, Thou bears witness to thyself; thy witness is not true. Jesus [25] answered and said unto them, If I bear witness to myself, my witness is true; for I know whence I came, and whither I go; but ye know not whence I came, or [26, 27] whither I go. And ye judge after the flesh; and I judge no man. And even if I judge, my judgement is true; because I am not alone, but I and my Father which [28, 29] sent me. And in your law it is written, that the witness of two men is true. I am he that bears witness to myself, and my Father which sent me bears witness to [30] me. They said unto him, Where is thy Father? Jesus answered and said

unto them, Ye know not me, nor my Father: for did ye know me, ye would know my [31] Father. He said these sayings in the treasury, where he was teaching in the [32] temple: and no man seized him; because his hour had not yet come. Jesus said unto them again, I go truly, and ye shall seek me and not find me, and ye shall die [33] in your sins: and where I go, ye cannot come. The Jews said, Will he haply kill [34] himself, that he said, Where I go, ye cannot come? He said unto them, Ye are from below; and I am from above: ye are of this world; and I am not of this [35] world. I said unto you, that ye shall die in your sins: if ye believe not that I am [36] he, ye shall die in your sins. The Jews said, And thou, who art thou? Jesus said [37] unto them, If I should begin to speak unto you, I have concerning you many words and judgement: but he that sent me is true; and I, what I heard from him is what [38, 39] I say in the world. And they knew not that he meant by that the Father. Jesus [Arabic, p. 135] said unto them again, When ye have lifted up the Son of man, then ye shall know that I am he: and I do nothing of myself, but as my Father [40] taught me, so I speak. And he that sent me is with me; and my Father hath not [41] left me alone; because I do what is pleasing to him at all times. And while he was saying that, many believed in him.

[42] And Jesus said to those Jews that believed in him, If ye abide in my words, truly [43] ye are my disciples; and ye shall know the truth, and the truth shall make you free. [44] They said unto him, We are the seed of Abraham, and have never served any man [45] in the way of slavery: how then says thou, Ye shall be free children? Jesus said unto them, Verily, verily, I say unto you, Everyone that doeth a sin is a slave of [46] sin. And the slave doth not remain forever in the house; but the son

remains [47, 48] forever. And if the Son set you free, truly ye shall be free children. I know that ye are the seed of Abraham; but ye seek to slay me, because ye are unable for my [49] word. And what I saw with my Father, I say: and what ye saw with your father, [50] ye do. They answered and said unto him, Our father is Abraham. Jesus said unto them, If ye were the children of Abraham, ye would do the deeds of Abraham. [51] Now, behold, ye seek to kill me, a man that speak with you the truth, that I [52] heard from God: this did Abraham not do. And ye do the deeds of your father. They said unto him, We were not *born* of fornication; we have one Father, who is [53] God. Jesus said unto them, If God were your Father, ye would love me: I proceeded and came from God; and it was not of my own self that I came, but he sent [54] [Arabic, p. 136] me. Why then do ye not know my word? Because ye cannot hear my word. [55] Ye are from the father, the devil, and the lust of your father do ye desire to do, who from the beginning is a slayer of men, and in the truth stands not, because the truth is not in him. And when he speaks untruth, he speaks from [56] himself: for he is a liar, and the father of untruth. And I who speak the truth, ye [57] believe me not. Who of you rebukes me for a sin? And if I speak the truth, ye [58] do not believe me. Whosoever is of God hears the words of God: therefore do [59] ye not hear, because ye are not of God. The Jews answered and said unto him, [60] Did we not say well that thou art a Samaritan, and hast demons? Jesus said unto them, As for me, I have not a devil; but my Father do I honor, and ye dishonor [61] me. I seek not my glory: here is one who seeks and judges.

Section XXXVI.

[1] Verily, verily, I say unto you, Whosoever kept my word shall not see death [2] forever. The Jews said unto him, Now we know that thou hast demons. Abraham is dead, and the prophets; and thou says, Whosoever kept my word shall not [3] taste death forever. Art thou haply greater than our father Abraham, who is [4] dead, and than the prophets, which are dead? Whom makes thou thyself? Jesus said unto them, If I glorify myself, my glory is nothing: my Father is he that [5] glorifies me; *of* whom ye say, that he is our God; and *yet* ye have not known him: but I know him; and if I should say that I know him not, I should become [6] [Arabic, p. 137] a liar like you: but I know him, and keep his word. Abraham your father [7] longed to see my day; and he saw, and rejoiced. The Jews said unto him, [8] Thou art now not fifty years old, and hast thou seen Abraham? Jesus said unto [9] them, Verily, verily, I say unto you, Before Abraham was, I am. And they take stones to stone him: but Jesus concealed himself, and went out of the temple. And he passed through them, and went *his way*.

[10] And as he passed, he saw a man blind from his mother's womb. And his [11] disciples asked him, and said, Our Master, who sinned, this *man*, or his parents, so [12] that he was born blind? Jesus said unto them, Neither did he sin, nor his parents: [13] but that the works of God may be seen in him. It is incumbent on me to do the deeds of him that sent me, while it is day: a night will come, and no man will be [14] able to busy himself. As long as I am in the world, I am the light of the world. [15] And when he said that, he spat upon the ground, and made clay of his spittle, and [16] smeared *it* on the eyes of the blind man, and said unto him, Go and wash thyself in [17] the pool of Siloam. And he went and washed, and came

seeing. And his neighbors, which saw him of old begging, said, Is not this he that was sitting begging? [18] And some said, It is he; and others said, Nay, but he resembles him much. He [19, 20] said, I am he. They said unto him, How then were thine eyes opened? He answered and said unto them, A man named Jesus made clay, and smeared *it* on my eyes, and said unto me, Go and wash in the water of Siloam: and I went and [21] washed, and received sight. They said unto him, Where is he? He said, I know not. [22, 23] [Arabic, p. 138] And they brought him that was previously blind to the Pharisees. And the day in which Jesus made clay and opened with it his eyes was a Sabbath [24] day. And again the Pharisees asked him, How didst thou receive sight? And he said [25] unto them, He put clay on mine eyes, and I washed, and received sight. The people of the Pharisees said, This man is not from God, for he kept not the Sabbath. And others said, How can a man *that is* a sinner do these signs? And there came [26] to be a division amongst them. And again they said to that blind man, Thou, then, what says thou of him that opened for thee thine eyes? He said unto them, [27] I say that he is a prophet. And the Jews did not believe concerning him, that he was blind, and received sight, until they summoned the parents of him who received [28] sight, and asked them, Is this your son, *of* whom ye said that he was born blind? [29] How then, behold, doth he now see? His parents answered and said, We know [30] that this is our son, and that he was born blind: but how he has come to see now, or who it is that opened his eyes, we know not: and he also has reached his prime; [31] ask him, and he will speak for himself. This said his parents, because they were fearing the Jews: and the Jews decided, that if any man should confess of him that [32] he was the Messiah, they would put him out of the synagogue. For this reason [33] said his parents, He hath reached his prime; ask him. And they called the man a second time, him that was blind, and said unto him, Praise God: we know that this [34] man is a sinner. He answered and said unto them, Whether he be a sinner, I know [35] not: I know one thing, that I was blind, and I now see. They said unto him again, [36] [Arabic, p. 139] What did he unto thee? How opened he for thee thine eyes? He said unto them, I said unto you, and ye did not hear: what wish ye further to hear? [37] Ye also, do ye wish to become disciples to him? And they reviled him, and said unto him, Thou art the disciple of that *man*; but as for us, we are the disciples of [38] Moses. And we know that God spoke unto Moses: but this man, we know not [39] whence he is. The man answered and said unto them, From this is the wonder, [40] because ye know not whence he is, and mine eyes hath he opened. And we know that God hears not the voice of sinners: but whosoever fears him, and does [41] his will, him he hears. From eternity hath it not been heard of, that a man [42] opened the eyes of a blind *man*, who had been born in blindness. If then this *man* [43] were not from God, he could not do that. They answered and said unto him, Thou was all of thee born in sins, and dost thou teach us? And they put him forth without.

[44] And Jesus heard of his being put forth without, and found him, and said unto [45] him, Does thou believe in the Son of God? He that was made whole answered [46] and said, Who is he, my Lord, that I may believe in him? Jesus said unto him, [47] Thou hast seen him, and he that speaks to thee is he. And he said, I believe, my Lord. And he fell down worshipping him.

Section XXXVII.

[1] And Jesus said, To judge the world am I come, so that they that see not may [2] see, and they that see may become blind. And some of the Pharisees which were [3] with him heard that, and they said unto him, Can it be that we are blind? Jesus said unto them, If ye were blind, ye should not have sin: but now ye say, We see: and because of this your sin remains.

[4] [Arabic, p. 140] Verily, verily, I say unto you, Whosoever enters not into the fold of the sheep by the door, but goes up from another place, that *man* is a thief and a [5, 6] stealer. But he that entered by the door is the shepherd of the sheep. And therefore the keeper of the door opened for him the door; and the sheep hear his voice: and [7] he called his sheep by their names, and they go forth unto him. And when he puts forth his sheep, he goes before them, and his sheep follow him: because [8] they know his voice. And after a stranger will the sheep not go, but they flee from [9] him: because they hear not the voice of a stranger. This parable spoke Jesus unto them: but they knew not what he was saying unto them.

[10] Jesus said unto them again, Verily, verily, I say unto you, I am the door of the [11] sheep. And all that came are thieves and stealers: but the sheep heard them not. [12] I am the door: and if a man enter by me, he shall live, and shall go in and go out, [13] and shall find pasture. And the stealer cometh not, save that he may steal, and kill, and destroy: but I came that they might have life, and that they might have [14] the thing *that is* better. I am the good shepherd; and the good shepherd giveth [15] himself for his sheep. But the hireling, who is not a shepherd, and whose the sheep are not, when he sees

the wolf as it cometh, leaves the sheep, and flees, [16] and the wolf cometh, and snatched away the sheep, and scattered them: and the [17] hireling flees because he is an hireling, and hath no care for the sheep. I am the [18] good shepherd; and I know what is mine, and what is mine knows me, as my Father knows me, and I know my Father; and I give myself for the sheep. [19] And I have other sheep also, that are not of this flock: them also I must invite, and they shall hear my voice; and all the sheep shall be one, and the shepherd one. [20] [Arabic, p. 141] And therefore doth my Father love me, because I give my life, that I may [21] take it again. No man taketh it from me, but I leave it of my own choice. And I have the right to leave it, and have the right also to take it. And this commandment did I receive of my Father.

[22] And there occurred a disagreement among the Jews because of these sayings. [23] And many of them said, He hath a devil, and is afflicted with madness; why listen [24] ye to him? And others said, These sayings are not those of *men* possessed with demons. Can a demon haply open the eyes of a blind *man?*

[25, 26] And the feast of the dedication came on at Jerusalem: and it was winter. And [27] Jesus was walking in the temple in the porch of Solomon. The Jews therefore surrounded him, and said unto him, Until when dost thou make our hearts anxious? [28] If thou art the Messiah, tell us plainly. He answered and said unto them, I told you, and ye believe not: and the deeds that I do in my Father's name bear witness [29, 30] to me. But ye believe not, because ye are not of my sheep, as I said unto you. [31] And my sheep hear my voice, and I know them, and they come after me: and I give them eternal life; and they shall not perish forever, nor shall any man snatch [32] them out

of my hands. For the Father, who hath given *them* unto me, is greater [33] than all; and no man is able to take *them* from the hand of my Father. And [34, 35] my Father are one. And the Jews took stones to stone him. Jesus said unto them, Many good deeds from my Father have I shewed you; because of which of them, [36] then, do ye stone me? The Jews said unto him, Not for the good deeds do we stone thee, but because thou blasphemes; and, whilst thou art a man, makes thyself [37] God. Jesus said unto them, Is it not thus written in your law, I said, Ye are gods? [38] [Arabic, p. 142] And if he called those gods— for to them came the word of God (and it is [39] not possible in the scripture that *anything* should be undone)—he then, whom the Father hath sanctified and sent into the world, do ye say that he blasphemes; [40] because I said unto you, I am the Son of God? If then I do not the deeds of my [41] Father, ye believe me not. But if I do, *even* if ye believe not me, believe the deeds: that ye may know and believe that my Father is in me, and I in my Father. [42] And they sought again to take him: and he went forth out of their hands.

[43] And he went beyond Jordan to the place where John was baptizing formerly; [44] and abode there. And many people came unto him; and they said, John did not [45] work even one sign: but all that John said of this man is truth. And many believed in him.

[46] And there was a sick *man*, named Lazarus, of the village of Bethany, the brother [47] of Mary and Martha. And Mary was she that anointed with sweet ointment the feet of Jesus, and wiped *them* with her hair; and Lazarus, who was sick, was the [48] brother of this *woman*. And his sisters sent unto Jesus, and said unto him, Our [49] Lord, behold, he whom thou loves is sick.

But Jesus said, This sickness is not unto death, but for the glorifying of God, that the Son of God may be glorified [50, 51] because of it. And Jesus loved Martha, and Mary, and Lazarus. And when he [52] heard that he was sick, he abode in the place where he was two days. And after that, [53] he said unto his disciples, Come, let us go into Judæa. His disciples said unto him, Our [Arabic, p. 143] Master, now the Jews desire to stone thee; and goes thou again thither? [54, 55] Jesus said unto them, Is not the day of twelve hours? If then a man walk in the day, he stumbles not, because he sees the light of the world. But if [56] a man walk in the night, he stumbles, because there is no lamp in him. This said Jesus: and after that, he said unto them, Lazarus our friend hath fallen asleep; but [57] I am going to awaken him. His disciples said unto him, Our Lord, if he hath [58] fallen asleep, he will recover. But Jesus said that concerning his death: while they [59] supposed that he spoke of lying down to sleep. Then Jesus said unto them plainly, [60] Lazarus is dead. And I am glad that I was not there for your sakes, that ye may [61] believe; but let us go thither. Thomas, who is called Thama, said to the disciples, his companions, Let us also go, and die with him.

Section XXXVIII.

[1, 2] And Jesus came to Bethany, and found him *already* four days in the grave. And Bethany was beside Jerusalem, and its distance from it *was* a sum of fifteen furlongs; [3] and many of the Jews came unto Mary and Martha, to comfort their heart [4] because of their brother. And Martha, when she heard that Jesus had come, went [5] out to meet him: but Mary was sitting in the house. Martha then said unto Jesus, [6] My Lord, if thou had

been here, my brother had not died. But I know now that, [7] whatever thou shalt ask of God, he will give thee. Jesus said unto her, Thy brother shall [8] rise. Martha said unto him, I know that he shall rise in the resurrection at the last day. [9] Jesus said unto her, I am the resurrection, and the life: whosoever believeth in [10] [Arabic, p. 144] me, even though he die, he shall live: and every living one that believeth [11] in me shall never die. Believes thou this? She said unto him, Yea, my Lord: I believe that thou art the Messiah, the Son of God, that cometh into the [12] world. And when she had said that, she went and called Mary her sister secretly, [13] and said unto her, Our Master hath come, and summoned thee. And Mary, when [14] she heard, rose in haste, and came unto him. (And Jesus then had not come into [15] the village, but was in the place where Martha met him.) And the Jews also that were with her in the house, to comfort her, when they saw that Mary rose up and went out in haste, went after her, because they supposed that she was going to the [16] tomb to weep. And Mary, when she came to where Jesus was, and saw him, fell at his feet, and said unto him, If thou had been here, my Lord, my brother had [17] not died. And Jesus came; and when he saw her weeping, and the Jews that were [18] with her weeping, he was troubled in himself, and sighed; and he said, In what [19] place have ye laid him? And they said unto him, Our Lord, come and see. And [20] the tears of Jesus came. The Jews therefore said, See the greatness of his love for [21] him! But some of them said, Could not this *man*, who opened the eyes of that [22] blind *man*, have caused that this *man* also should not die? And Jesus came to the place of burial, being troubled within himself. And the place of burial was a cave, [23] and a stone was placed at its door.

Jesus therefore said, Take these stones *away*. Martha, the sister of him *that was* dead, said unto him, My Lord, he hath come to [24] stink for some time: he hath been four days *dead*. Jesus said unto her, Did not I say [25] [Arabic, p. 145] unto thee, If thou believes, thou shalt see the glory of God? And they removed those stones. And Jesus lifted his eyes on high, and said, My Father, [26] I thank thee since thou didst hear me. And I know that thou at all times hears me: but I say this unto thee because of this multitude that is standing, that they [27] may believe that thou didst send me. And when he had said that, he cried with a [28] loud voice, Lazarus, come forth. And that dead *man* came out, having his hands and feet bound with bandages, and his face wrapped in a scarf. Jesus said unto them, Loose him, and let him go.

[29] And many of the Jews which came unto Mary, when they saw the deed of Jesus, [30] believed in him. But some of them went to the Pharisees, and informed them of all that Jesus did.

[31] And the chief priests and the Pharisees gathered, and said, What shall we do? [32] For lo, this man doeth many signs. And if we leave him thus, all men will believe [33] in him: and the Romans will come and take our country and people. And one of them, who was called Caiaphas, the chief priest he was in that year, said unto them, [34] Ye know not anything, nor consider that it is more advantageous for us that one [35] man should die instead of the people, and not that the whole people perish. And this he said not of himself: but because he was the chief priest of that year, he [36] prophesied that Jesus was to die instead of the people; and not instead of the people alone, but that he might gather the scattered

children of God together. [37] And from that day they considered *how* to kill him.

[38] [Arabic, p. 146] And Jesus did not walk openly amongst the Jews, but departed thence to a place near the wilderness, to a town called Ephraim; and he was there, going [39] about with his disciples. And the Passover of the Jews was near: and many went [40] up from the villages unto Jerusalem before the feast, to purify themselves. And they sought for Jesus, and said one to another in the temple, What think ye of his [41] holding back from the feast? And the chief priests and the Pharisees had given commandment, that, if any man knew in what place he was, he should reveal *it* to them, that they might take him.

[42] And when the days of his going up were accomplished, he prepared himself that [43] he might go to Jerusalem. And he sent messengers before him, and departed, and [44] entered into a village of Samaria, that they might make ready for him. And they [45] received him not, because he was prepared for going to Jerusalem. And when James and John his disciples saw *it*, they said unto him, Our Lord, wilt thou that we speak, and fire come down from heaven, to extirpate them, as did Elijah also? [46] And Jesus turned, and rebuked them, and said, Ye know not of what spirit ye are. [47] Verily the Son of man did not come to destroy lives, but to give life. And they went to another village.

Section XXXIX.

[1] And Jesus six days before the Passover came to Bethany, where was Lazarus, [2] whom Jesus raised from among the dead. And they made a feast for him there: [3] and Martha was serving; while Lazarus was one

of them that sat with him. And [4] at the time of Jesus' being at Bethany in the house of Simon the leper, great multitudes of the Jews heard that Jesus was there: and they came, not because of Jesus alone, but [Arabic, p. 147] that they might look also on Lazarus, whom he raised from among the dead. [5, 6] And the chief priests considered *how* they might kill Lazarus also; because [7] many of the Jews were going on his account, and believing in Jesus. And Mary took a case of the ointment of fine nard, of great price, and opened it, and poured [8] it out on the head of Jesus as he was reclining; and she anointed his feet, and wiped them with her hair: and the house was filled with the odor of the ointment. [9, 10] But Judas Iscariot, one of the disciples, he that was to betray him, said, Why was [11] not this ointment sold for three hundred pence, and given unto the poor? This he said, not because of his care for the poor, but because he was a thief, and the chest [12] was with him, and what was put into it he used to bear. And that displeased the rest of the disciples also within themselves, and they said, Why went this ointment [13] to waste? It was possible that it should be sold for much, and the poor be given [14] it. And they were angry with Mary. And Jesus perceived *it*, and said unto them, Leave her; why molest ye her? A good work hath she accomplished on me: for the [15] day of my burial kept she it. At all times the poor are with you, and when ye [16] wish ye can do them a kindness: but I am not at all times with you. And for this *cause*, when she poured this ointment on my body, it is as if she did it for my burial, [17] and anointed my body beforehand. And verily I say unto you, In every place where this my gospel shall be proclaimed in all the world, what she did shall be told for a memorial of her.

[18, 19] [Arabic, p. 148] And when Jesus said that, he went out leisurely to go to Jerusalem. And when he arrived at Bethphage and at Bethany, beside the mount which is [20] called the mount of Olives, Jesus sent two of his disciples, and he said unto them, Go [21] into this village that is opposite you: 2683and when ye enter it, ye shall find an ass tied, and [22] a colt with him, which no man ever yet mounted: loose him, and bring them unto me. And if any man say unto you, Why loose ye them? Say unto him thus, We [23] seek them for our Lord; and straightway send them hither. All this was, that what was said in the prophet might be fulfilled, which said,

[24] Say ye unto the daughter of Zion,
Behold, thy King cometh unto thee,
Meek, and riding upon an ass,
And upon a colt the foal of an ass.

[25] And the disciples did not know this at that time: but after that Jesus was glorified, his disciples remembered that these *things* were written of him, and *that* this [26] they had done unto him. And when the two disciples went, they found as he had [27] said unto them, and they did as Jesus charged them. And when they loosed them, [28] their owners said unto them, Why loose ye them? They said unto them, We seek [29] them for our Lord. And they let them *go*. And they brought the ass and the colt, [30] and they placed on the colt their garments; and Jesus mounted it. And most of the multitudes spread their garments on the ground before him: and others cut branches [31] from the trees, and threw *them* in the way. And when he neared his descent from [Arabic, p. 149] the mount of Olives, all the disciples began to rejoice and to praise God with [32] a loud voice for all the powers

which they had seen; and they said, Praise in the highest; Praise to the Son of David: Blessed is he that cometh in the name [33] of the Lord; and blessed is the kingdom that cometh, *that* of our father David: Peace in heaven, and praise in the highest.

[34] And a great multitude, that which came to the feast, when they heard that Jesus [35] was coming to Jerusalem, took young palm branches, and went forth to meet him, and cried and said, Praise: Blessed is he that cometh in the name of the Lord, the [36] King of Israel. Certain therefore of the Pharisees from among the multitudes [37] said unto him, Our Master, rebuke thy disciples. He said unto them, Verily I say unto you, If these were silent, the stones would cry out.

[38, 39] And when he drew near, and saw the city, he wept over it, and said, Would that thou had known the things that are for thy peace, in this thy day! Now that is [40] hidden from thine eyes. There shall come unto thee days when thine enemies [41] shall encompass thee, and straiten thee from every quarter, and shall get possession of thee, and thy children within thee; and they shall not leave in thee a stone upon another; because thou knew not the time of thy visitation.

[42] And when he entered into Jerusalem, the whole city was agitated, and they said, [43] Who is this? And the multitudes said, This is Jesus, the prophet that is from Nazareth [44] of Galilee. And the multitude which was with him bare witness that he called [45] Lazarus from the grave, and raised him from among the dead. And for this *cause* great multitudes went out to meet him, because they heard the sign which he did.

Section XL.

[1] [Arabic, p. 150] And when Jesus entered the temple, they brought unto him blind and [2] lame: and he healed them. But when the chief priests and the Pharisees saw the wonders that he did, and the children that were crying in the temple and [3] saying, Praise be to the Son of David: it distressed them, and they said, Hears thou not what these say? Jesus said unto them, Yea: did ye not read long ago, From [4] the mouths of children and infants thou hast chosen my praise? And the Pharisees said one to another, Behold, do ye not see that nothing availed us? For lo, the whole world hath followed him.

[5] And there were among them certain Gentiles also, which had come up to worship [6] at the feast: these therefore came to Philip, who was of Bethsaida of Galilee, [7] and asked him, and said unto him, My lord, we wish to see Jesus. And Philip [8] came and told Andrew: and Andrew and Philip told Jesus. And Jesus answered and said unto them, The hour is come nigh, in which the Son of man is to be glorified. [9] Verily, verily, I say unto you, A grain of wheat, if it fall not and die in the [10] earth, remains alone; but if it die, it bears much fruit. He that loves his life destroys it; and he that hated his life in this world shall keep it unto the life eternal. [11] If a man serve me, he will follow me; and where I am, there shall my servant be [12] also: and whosoever serves me, the Father will honor him. Now is my soul troubled: [Arabic, p. 151] and what shall I say? My Father, deliver me from this hour. But [13] for this cause came I unto this hour. My Father, glorify thy name. And a [14] voice was heard from heaven, I have glorified *it*, and shall glorify *it*. And the multitude that were standing heard, and said, This is thunder: and others said, An [15] angel speaks to him. Jesus answered and said unto them, Not because of

me [16] was this voice, but because of you. Now is the judgement of this world; and the [17] prince of this world shall now be cast forth. And I, when I am lifted up from the [18] earth, shall draw every man unto me. This he said, that he might shew by what [19] manner of death he should die. The multitudes said unto him, We have heard out of the law that the Messiah abides forever: how then says thou, that the Son of [20] man is to be lifted up? Who is this, the Son of man? Jesus said unto them, Another little while is the light with you. Walk so long as ye have light, lest the darkness overtake you; for he that walks in the darkness knows not whither he goes. [21] So long as ye have light, believe the light, that ye may be the children of the light.

[22] And when certain of the Pharisees asked of Jesus, when the kingdom of God should come, he answered and said unto them, The kingdom of God cometh not [23] with expectation: neither shall they say, Lo, it is here! Nor, Lo, it is there! For the kingdom of God is within you.

[24] And in the day*time* he was teaching in the temple; and at night he used to go [25] out, and pass the night in the mount called the Mount of Olives. And all the people came to him in the morning in the temple, to hear his word.

[26, 27] Then spoke Jesus unto the multitudes and his disciples, and said unto them, On [28] [Arabic, p. 152] the seat of Moses are seated the scribes and Pharisees: everything that they say unto you now to keep, keep and do: but according to their deeds [29] do ye not; for they say, and do not. And they bind heavy burdens, and lay them on the shoulders of the people; while they with one of their fingers will not come [30, 31] near them. But all

their deeds they do to make a shew before men. And all the multitude were hearing that with pleasure.

[32] And in the course of his teaching he said unto them, Guard yourselves from the [33] scribes, who desire to walk in robes, and love salutation in the marketplaces, and sitting in the highest places of the synagogues, and at feasts in the highest parts of [34] the rooms: and they broaden their amulets, and lengthen the cords of their cloaks, [35] and *love* that they should be called by men, My master, and devour widows' houses, because of their prolonging their prayers; these then shall receive greater judgement. [36] But ye, be ye not called masters: for your master is one; all ye are brethren. [37] Call not then to yourselves *any one* father on earth: for your Father is one, who is [38] in heaven. And be not called directors: for your director is one, *even* the Messiah. [39, 40] He that is great among you shall be unto you a minister. Whosoever shall exalt himself shall be abased; and whosoever shall abase himself shall be exalted.

[41] Woe unto you, Pharisees! Because ye love the highest places in the synagogues, and salutation in the marketplaces.

[42] Woe unto you, scribes and Pharisees, hypocrites! Because ye devour widows' houses, because of your prolonging your prayers: for this *reason* then ye shall receive greater judgement.

[43] Woe unto you, scribes and Pharisees, hypocrites! Because ye have shut the kingdom of God before men.

[44] [Arabic, p. 153] Woe unto you that know the law! For ye concealed the keys of knowledge: ye enter not, and those that are entering ye suffer not to enter.

[45] Woe unto you, scribes and Pharisees, hypocrites! Because ye compass land and sea to draw one proselyte; and when he is *become so*, ye make him a son of hell twice as much as yourselves.

[46] Woe unto you, ye blind guides! Because ye say, Whosoever swears by the temple, it is nothing; but whosoever swears by the gold that is in the temple, [47] shall be condemned. Ye blind foolish *ones*: which is greater, the gold, or the [48] temple which sanctifies the gold? And, Whosoever swears by the altar, it is nothing; but whosoever swears by the offering that is upon it, shall be condemned. [49] Ye blind foolish *ones*: which is greater, the offering, or the altar which sanctifies [50] the offering? Whosoever then swears by the altar, hath sworn by it, and by all [51] that is upon it. And whosoever swears by the temple, hath sworn by it, and by [52] him that is dwelling in it. And whosoever swears by heaven, hath sworn by the throne of God, and by him that sits upon it.

[53] Woe unto you, scribes and Pharisees, hypocrites! Because ye tithe mint and rue and dill and cummin and all herbs, and ye leave the important *matters* of the law, judgement, and mercy, and faith, and the love of God: this ought ye to do, and [54] not to leave that *undone*. Ye blind guides, which strain out a gnat, and swallow camels.

[55] Woe unto you, scribes and Pharisees, hypocrites! Because ye cleanse the outside of the cup and of the platter, while the inside of them is full of injustice and wrong. [56] Ye blind Pharisees, cleanse first the inside of the cup and of the platter, then shall the outside of them be cleansed.

[57] [Arabic, p. 154] Woe unto you, scribes and Pharisees, hypocrites! Because ye resemble whited sepulchers, which appear from the outside beautiful, but within [58] full of the bones of the dead, and all uncleanness. So ye also from without appear unto men like the righteous, but within ye are full of wrong and hypocrisy.

[59] One of the scribes answered and said unto him, Teacher, in this saying of thine [60] thou art casting a slur on us. He said, And to you also, ye scribes, woe! For ye lade men with heavy burdens, and ye with one of your fingers come not near those burdens.

[61] Woe unto you, scribes and Pharisees, hypocrites! For ye build the tombs of the prophets, which your fathers killed, and adorn the burying-places of the righteous, [62] and say, If we had been in the days of our fathers, we should not have been partakers [63] with them in the blood of the prophets. Wherefore, behold, ye witness against [64] yourselves, that ye are the children of those that slew the prophets. And ye also, [65] ye fill up the measure of your fathers. Ye serpents, ye children of vipers, where shall ye flee from the judgement of Gehenna?

Section XLI.

[1] Therefore, behold, I, the wisdom of God, am sending unto you prophets, and apostles, and wise men, and scribes: and some of them ye shall slay and crucify; and some of them ye shall beat in your synagogues, and persecute from city to [2] city: that there may come on you all the blood of the righteous that hath been poured upon the ground from the blood of Abel the pure to the blood of Zachariah the son of Barachiah, whom ye slew

between the temple and the altar. [3] Verily I say unto you, All these *things* shall come upon this generation.

[4] [Arabic, p. 155] O Jerusalem, Jerusalem, slayer of the prophets, and stoner of them that are sent unto her! How many times did I wish to gather thy children, as [5] a hen gathered her chickens under her wings, and ye would not! Your house shall [6] be left over you desolate. Verily I say unto you, Ye shall not see me henceforth, till ye shall say Blessed is he that cometh in the name of the Lord.

[7] And many of the rulers also believed on him; but because of the Pharisees they [8] were not confessing *him*, lest they be put out of the synagogue: and they loved [9] the praise of men more than the praising of God. And Jesus cried and said, [10] Whosoever believeth in me, believeth not in me, but in him that sent me. And [11] whosoever sees me hath seen him that sent me. I am come a light into the [12] world, and so everyone that believeth in me abides not in the darkness. And whosoever hears my sayings, and kept them not, I judge him not: for I came [13] not to judge the world, but to give the world life. Whosoever wronged me, and receives not my sayings, there is one that judges him: the word that I spoke, it [14] shall judge him at the last day. I from myself did not speak: but the Father which sent me, he hath given me commandment, what I should say, and what I [15] should speak; and I know that his commandment is eternal life. The things that I say now, as my Father hath said unto me, *even* so I say.

[16] And when he said that unto them, the scribes and Pharisees began their evildoing, being angry with *him*, and finding fault with his sayings, and harassing him [17] in many things; 2828seeking to catch something

from his mouth, that they might be able to calumniate him.

[18] And when there gathered together myriads of great multitudes, which almost trode [Arabic, p. 156] one upon another, Jesus began to say unto his disciples, Preserve yourselves [19] from the leaven of the Pharisees, which is hypocrisy. For there is nothing [20] concealed, that shall not be revealed: nor hid, that shall not be known. Everything that ye have said in the darkness shall be heard in the light; and what ye have spoken secretly in the ears in the inner chambers shall be proclaimed on the roofs.

[21, 22] This said Jesus, and he went and hid himself from them. But notwithstanding [23] his having done all these signs before them, they believed not in him: that the word of Isaiah the prophet might be fulfilled, who said,

My Lord, who is he that hath believed to hear us?

And the arm of the Lord, to whom hath it appeared?

[24] And for this reason it is not possible for them to believe, because Isaiah also said,

[25] They have blinded their eyes, and made dark their heart;

That they may not see with their eyes, and understand with their heart,

And turn,

So that I should heal them.

[26] This said Isaiah when he saw his glory, and spoke of him.

[27] And when Jesus went out of the temple, certain of his disciples came forward

[28] to show him the buildings of the temple, and its beauty and greatness, and the strength of the stones that were laid in it, and the elegance of its building, and that [29] it was adorned with noble stones and beautiful colors. Jesus answered and said [30] unto them, See ye these great buildings? Verily I say unto you, Days will come, when there shall not be left here a stone upon another, that shall not be cast down.

[31] And two days before the Passover of unleavened bread, the chief priests and [32] the scribes sought how they might take him by deceit, and kill him: and they said, It shall not be at the feast, lest the people be agitated.

[33] And when Jesus sat on the mount of Olives opposite the temple, his disciples, Simon Cephas and James and John and Andrew, came forward unto him, and said unto him [34] between themselves and him, Teacher, tell us when that shall be, and what is the sign [35] [Arabic, p. 157] of thy coming and the end of the world. Jesus answered and said unto them, Days will come, when ye shall long to see one of the days of the Son of [36, 37] man, and shall not behold. Take heed lest any man lead you astray. Many shall [38] come in my name, and say, I am the Messiah; and they shall say, The time is come [39] near, and shall lead many astray: go not therefore after them. And when ye hear of wars and tidings of insurrections, see *to it*, be not agitated: for these *things* must [40] first be; only the end is not yet come. Nation shall rise against nation, and kingdom [41] against kingdom: and great earthquakes shall be in one place and another, and there shall be famines and deaths and agitations: and there shall be fear and terror and great

signs that shall appear from heaven, and there shall be great [42, 43] storms All these *things* are the beginning of travail. But before all of that, they shall lay hands upon you, and persecute you, and deliver you unto the synagogues [44] and into prisons, and bring you before kings and judges for my name's sake. And [45] that shall be unto you for a witness. But first must my gospel be preached unto all [46] nations. And when they bring you into the synagogues before the rulers and the authorities, be not anxious beforehand how ye shall answer for yourselves, or what ye [47, 48] shall say: because it is not ye that speak, but the Holy Spirit. Lay it to your heart, not [49] [Arabic, p. 158] to be anxious before the time what ye shall say: and I shall give you understanding and wisdom, which all your adversaries shall not be able to gainsay. [50] And then shall they deliver you unto constraint, and shall kill you: and ye shall be [51] hated of all nations because of my name. And then shall many go astray, and they [52] shall hate one another, and deliver one another unto death. And your parents, and your brethren, and your kinsfolk, and your friends shall deliver you up, and shall [53, 54] slay some of you. But a lock of hair from your heads shall not perish. And by [55] your patience ye shall gain your souls. And many *men*, false prophets, shall arise, [56] and lead many astray. And because of the abounding of iniquity, the love of many [57] shall wax cold. But he that endures to the end, the same shall be saved. And [58] this, the gospel of the kingdom, shall be preached in all the world for a testimony to all nations; and then shall come the end of all.

Section XLII.

[1] But when ye see Jerusalem with the army compassing it about, then know that [2] its desolation is come near. Those then that are in Judæa at that time shall flee to the mountain; and those that are within her shall flee; and those that are in the [3] villages shall not enter her. For these days are the days of vengeance, that all that [4] is written may be fulfilled. And when ye see the unclean sign of desolation, spoken of in Daniel the prophet, standing in the pure place, he that reads shall understand, [5, 6] and then he that is in Judæa shall flee in to the mountain: and let him that is on the [7] roof not go down, nor enter in to take anything from his house: and let him that is in [8] [Arabic, p. 159] the field not turn behind him to take his garment. Woe to them that are with child and to them that give suck in those days! There shall be great [9] distress in the land, and wrath against this nation. And they shall fall on the edge of the sword, and shall be taken captive to every land: and Jerusalem shall be trodden down of the nations, until the times of the nations be ended.

[10] Then if any man say unto you, The Messiah is here; or, Lo, he is there; believe [11] him not: there shall rise then false Messiahs and prophets of lying, and shall do signs and wonders, in order that they may lead astray even the elect also, if they [12] be able. But as for you, beware: for I have acquainted you with everything [13] beforehand. If then they say unto you, Lo, he is in the desert; go not out, lest ye [14] be taken: and if they say unto you, Lo, he is in the chamber; believe not. And as the lightning appears from the east, and is seen unto the west; so shall be the [15] coming of the Son of man. But first he must suffer much and be rejected by this [16] generation. Pray therefore that your flight be not in

winter, nor on a Sabbath: [17] there shall be then great tribulation, the like of which there hath not been from the [18] beginning of the world till now, nor shall be. And except the Lord had shortened those days, no flesh would have lived: but because of the elect, whom he elected, [19] he shortened those days. And there shall be signs in the sun and the moon and the stars; and upon the earth affliction of the nations, and rubbing of hands for the confusion [20] [Arabic, p. 160] of the noise of the sea, and an earthquake: the souls of men shall [21] go forth from fear of that which is to come upon the earth. And in those days, straightway after the distress of those days, the sun shall become dark, and the moon shall not shew its light, and the stars shall fall from heaven, and the powers [22] of heaven shall be convulsed: and then shall appear the sign of the Son of man in heaven: and at that time all the tribes of the earth shall wail, and look unto the Son [23] of man coming on the clouds of heaven with power and much glory. And he shall send his angels with the great trumpet, and they shall gather his elect from the four [24] winds, from one end of heaven to the other. But when these things begin to be, be of good cheer, and lift up your heads; for your salvation is come near.

[25] Learn the example of the fig tree: when it lets down its branches, and puts [26] forth its leaves, ye know that the summer is come; so ye also, when ye see these things begun to be, know ye that the kingdom of God hath arrived at the [27] door. Verily I say unto you, This generation shall not pass away, until all these [28] *things* shall be. Heaven and earth shall pass away, but my sayings shall not pass away.

[29] Take heed to yourselves, that your hearts become not heavy with inordinate desire, and

drunkenness, and the care of the world at any time, and that day come [30] upon you suddenly: for it is as a shock that shocks all the inhabitants that are on the [31] face of the whole earth. Watch at all times, and pray, that ye may be worthy to escape [Arabic, p. 161] from all the things that are to be, and that ye may stand before the Son of [32] man. Of that day and of that hour hath no man learned, not even the angels [33] of heaven, neither the Son, but the Father. See ye, and watch and pray: for ye know [34] not when that time *will be*. *It is* as a man, who journeyed, and left his house, and gave his authority to his servants, and appointed every man to his work, and [35] charged the porter to be wakeful. Be wakeful then: since ye know not when the lord of the house comes, in the evening, or in the middle of the night, or when the [36] cock crows, or in the morning; lest he come unexpectedly, and find you sleeping. [37] The thing that I say unto you, unto all of you do I say it, Be ye watchful.

[38] For as it was in the days of Noah, so shall the coming of the Son of man be. [39] As they were before the flood eating and drinking, and taking wives, and giving [40] wives to men, until the day in which Noah entered into the ark, and they perceived not till the flood came, and took them all; so shall the coming of the Son of man [41] be. And as it was in the days of Lot; they were eating and drinking, and selling [42] and buying, and planting and building, on the day in which Lot went out from Sodom, and the Lord rained fire and brimstone from heaven, and destroyed them [43, 44] all: so shall it be in the day in which the Son of man is revealed. And in that day, whosoever is on the roof, and his garments in the house, let him not go down to [45] take them: and he that is in the field shall not turn behind him. Remember Lot's

[46] wife. Whosoever shall desire to save his life shall destroy it: but whosoever shall [47] destroy his life shall save it. Verily I say unto you, In that night there shall be two on [48] [Arabic, p. 162] one bed; one shall be taken, and another left. And two *women* shall be grinding [49] at one mill; one shall be taken, and another left. And two shall be in the [50] field; one shall be taken, and another left. They answered and said unto him, To what place, our Lord? He said unto them, Where the body is, there will the eagles [51, 52] gather. Be attentive now: for ye know not at what hour your Lord cometh. Know this: if the master of the house had known in what watch the thief would come, he would have been attentive, and would not make it possible that his house should be [53] broken through. Therefore be ye also ready: for in the hour that ye think not the Son of man cometh.

Section XLIII.

[1] Simon Cephas said unto him, Our Lord, *is it* to us *that* thou hast spoken this [2] parable, or also to every man? Jesus said unto him, Who, thinks thou, is the servant, the master of the house, trusted with control, whom his lord set over his [3] household, to give them their food in its season? Blessed is that servant, whom his [4] lord shall come and find having done so. Verily I say unto you, He will set him [5] over all that he hath. But if that evil servant say in his heart, My lord delayed his [6] coming; and shall begin to beat his servants and the maidservants of his lord, and [7] shall begin to eat and to drink with the drunken; the lord of that servant shall come [8] in the day that he think not, and in the hour that he knows not, and shall [Arabic, p. 163] judge him, and appoint his portion with the hypocrites, and with those

that are not faithful: there shall be weeping and gnashing of teeth.

[9] Then shall the kingdom of heaven be like unto ten virgins, those that took their [10] lamps, and went forth to meet the bridegroom and the bride. Five of them were [11] wise, and five foolish. And those foolish *ones* took their lamps, and took not with [12, 13] them oil: but those wise *ones* took oil in vessels along with their lamps. When then [14] the bridegroom delayed, they all slumbered and slept. But in the middle of the night there occurred a cry, Behold, the bridegroom cometh! Go forth therefore to [15, 16] meet him. Then all those virgins arose, and made ready their lamps. The foolish [17] said unto the wise, Give us of your oil; for our lamps are gone out. But those wise answered and said, Perhaps there will not be enough for us and you: but go ye to [18] the sellers, and buy for yourselves. And when they went away to buy, the bridegroom came; and those that were ready went in with him to the marriage feast: and [19] the door was shut. And at last those other virgins also came and said, Our Lord, [20] our Lord, open unto us. He answered and said unto them, Verily I say unto you, [21] I know you not. Watch then, for ye know not that day nor that hour.

[22] *It is* as a man, who went on a journey, and called his servants, and delivered unto [23] them his possessions. And unto one he gave five talents, and another two, and another [24] one; everyone according to his strength; and went on *his* journey forthwith. He [Arabic, p. 164] then that received the five talents went and traded with them, and gained [26] other five. And so also he of the two gained other two. But he that received [27] the one went and digged in the earth, and hid the money of his lord. And after a long time the lord of those

servants came, and took from them the account. [28] And he that received five talents came near and brought other five, and said, My lord, thou gives me five talents: lo, I have gained other five in addition to them. [29] His lord said unto him, Well done, thou good and faithful servant: over a little hast [30] thou been faithful, over much will I set thee: enter into the joy of thy lord. And he that had the two came near and said, My lord, thou gives me two talents: lo, [31] other two have I gained in addition to them. His lord said unto him, Good, thou faithful servant: over a little hast thou been faithful, over much will I set thee: enter [32] into the joy of thy lord. And he also that received the one talent came forward and said, My lord, I knew thee that thou art a severe man, who reaps where thou [33] sows not, and gathers where thou didst not scatter: and so I was afraid, and [34] went away and hid thy talent in the earth: lo, thou hast what is thine. His lord answered and said unto him, Thou wicked and slothful servant, thou knew me [35] that I reap where I sowed not, and gather where I did not scatter; it was incumbent on thee to put my money to the bank, and *then* I should come and seek it with its [36] gains. Take now from him the talent, and give it to him that hath ten talents. [37] Whosoever hath shall be given, and he shall have more: but he that hath not, even [38] [Arabic, p. 165] what he hath shall be taken from him. And the unprofitable servant, put him forth into the outer darkness: there shall be the weeping and gnashing of teeth.

[39, 40] Your loins shall be girded, and your lamps lit; and ye shall be like the people that are looking for their lord, when he shall return from the feast; so that, when [41] he comes and knocks, they may at once open unto him. Blessed are those servants, whom their lord

shall come and find attentive: verily I say unto you, that he will gird his waist, and make them sit down, and pass through *them* and serve [42] them. And if he come in the second watch, or the third, and find thus, blessed are those servants.

[43] But when the Son of man cometh in his glory, and all his pure angels with him, [44] then shall he sit on the throne of his glory: and he will gather before him all the nations, and separate them the one from the other, like the shepherd who separates [45] the sheep from the goats; and will set the sheep on his right, and the goats on his [46] left. Then shall the King say to those that are at his right, Come, ye blessed of my Father, inherit the kingdom prepared for you from the foundations of the world: [47] I hungered, and ye gave me to eat; and I thirsted, and ye gave me to drink; and I [48] was a stranger, and ye took me in; 3005and I was naked, and ye clothed me; and I [49] was sick, and ye visited me; and I was in prison, and ye cared for me. Then shall those righteous say unto him, Our Lord, when saw we thee hungry, and fed thee? [50] Or thirsty, and gave thee to drink? And when saw we thee a stranger, and took [51] thee in? Or naked, and clothed thee? And when saw we thee sick, or imprisoned, and [52] cared for thee? The King shall answer and say unto them, Verily I say unto you, What [53] [Arabic, p. 166] ye did to one of these my brethren, the little ones, ye did unto me. Then shall he say unto those that are on his left also, Depart from me, ye cursed, [54] into the eternal fire prepared for the devil and his hosts: I hungered, and ye fed me [55] not; and I thirsted, and ye did not give me to drink; and I was a stranger, and ye took me not in; and I was naked, and ye clothed me not; and I was sick, and imprisoned, [56] and ye visited me not. Then shall those

also answer and say, Our Lord, when saw we thee a hungered, or athirst, or naked, or a stranger, or sick, or imprisoned, [57] and did not minister unto thee? Then shall he answer and say unto them, Verily I say unto you, When ye did *it* not unto one of these little *ones*, ye did *it* not [58] unto me also. And these shall go away into eternal punishment: but the righteous into eternal life.

Section XLIV.

[1, 2] And when Jesus finished all these sayings, he said unto his disciples, Ye know that after two days will be the Passover, and the Son of man is delivered up to be [3] crucified. Then gathered together the chief priests, and the scribes, and the elders [4] of the people, unto the court of the chief priest, who was called Caiaphas; and they took counsel together concerning Jesus, that they might seize him by subtlety, and [5] kill him. But they said, Not during the feast, lest there take place a disturbance among the people; for they feared the people.

[6] And Satan entered into Judas who was called Iscariot, who was of the number [7] of the twelve. And he went away, and communed with the chief priests, and the scribes, and those that held command in the temple, and said unto them, What [8] [Arabic, p. 167] would ye pay me, and I will deliver him unto you? And they, when they heard *it*, were pleased, and made ready for him thirty *pieces* of money. [9] And he promised them, and from that time he sought an opportunity that he might deliver unto them Jesus without the multitude.

[10] And on the first day of unleavened bread the disciples came to Jesus, and said unto him, Where wilt thou that we go and make ready for thee that thou may eat the Passover?

[11] And before the feast of the Passover, Jesus knew that the hour was arrived for his departure from this world unto his Father; and he loved his own in this world, [12] and to the last he loved them. And at the time of the feast, Satan put into the [13] heart of Judas, the son of Simon Iscariot, to deliver him up. And Jesus, because he knew that the Father had delivered into his hands everything, and that he came [14] forth from the Father, and goes unto God, rose from supper, and laid *aside* his [15] garments; and took a towel, *and* girded his waist, and poured water into a basin, and began to wash the feet of his disciples, and to wipe them with the towel wherewith [16] his waist was girded. And when he came to Simon Cephas, Simon said unto [17] him, Does thou, my Lord, wash for me my feet? Jesus answered and said unto [18] him, What I do, now thou knows not; but afterwards thou shalt learn. Simon said unto him, Thou shalt never wash for me my feet. Jesus said unto him, If I [19] wash thee not, thou hast no part with me. Simon Cephas said unto him, Then, my [20] Lord, wash not for me my feet alone, but my hands also and my head. Jesus said unto him, He that bathed needed not to wash save his feet, whereas his whole [21] *body* is clean: and ye also are clean, but not all of you. For Jesus knew him that should betray him; therefore said he, Ye are not all clean.

[22] [Arabic, p. 168] So when he had washed their feet, he took his garments, and sat down, and [23] said unto them, Know ye what I have done unto you? Ye call me, Master, [24] and, Lord: and ye say well; so I am. If

then I, now, who am your Lord and Master, have washed for you your feet, how needful is it that ye should wash one another's feet! [25] This have I given you as an example, that as I have done to you so ye should do [26] also. Verily, verily, I say unto you, No servant is greater than his lord; nor an [27] apostle greater than he that sent him. If ye know that, ye are happy if ye do it. [28] My saying this is not for all of you: for I know whom I have chosen: but that the scripture might be fulfilled, He that eats with me bread lifted against me his [29] heel. Henceforth I say unto you before it come to pass, that, when it cometh to [30] pass, ye may believe that I am *he*. Verily, verily, I say unto you, Whosoever receives whomsoever I send receives me; and whosoever receives me receives him that sent me.

[31] Who is the great *one*, he that sits, or he that serves? Is it not he that sits? [32] I am among you as he that serves. But ye are they that have continued with me [33] in my temptations; I promise you, as my Father promised me, the kingdom, that ye may eat and drink at the table of my kingdom.

[34] And the first day came, the feast of unleavened bread, on which the Jews were [35] wont to sacrifice the Passover. And Jesus sent two of his disciples, Cephas and John, and said unto them, Go and make ready for us the Passover, that we may eat. [36, 37] And they said unto him, Where wilt thou that we make ready for thee? He said unto them, Go, enter the city; and at the time of your entering, there shall meet you a man bearing a pitcher of water; follow him, and the place where he entered, say [38] to such an one, the master of the house, Our Master said, My time is come, and [Arabic, p. 169] at thy *house* I keep the Passover. Where then is the lodging-

place where [39] I shall eat with my disciples? And he will shew you a large upper room [40] spread and made ready: there then make ready for us. And his two disciples went out, and came to the city, and found as he had said unto them: and they made ready the Passover as he had said unto them.

[41] And when the evening was come, and the time arrived, Jesus came and reclined, [42] and the twelve apostles with him. And he said unto them, With desire I have [43] desired to eat this Passover with you before I suffer: I say unto you, that henceforth I shall not eat it, until it is fulfilled in the kingdom of God.

[44] Jesus said that, and was agitated in his spirit, and testified, and said, Verily, [45] verily, I say unto you, One of you, *he* that eats with me, shall betray me. And they were very sorrowful; and they began to say unto him, one after another of [46] them, Can it be I, Lord? He answered and said unto them, One of the twelve, [47] he that dips his hand with me in the dish, will betray me. And lo, the hand of [48] him that betrays me is on the table. And the Son of man goes, as it is written of him: woe then to that man by whose hand the Son of man is betrayed! For it [49] would have been better for that man had he not been born. And the disciples [50] looked one on another, for they knew not to whom he referred; and they began to search among themselves, who that might be who was to do *this*.

Section XLV.
[1, 2] [Arabic, p. 170] And one of his disciples was sitting in his bosom, *he* whom Jesus loved. To him Simon Cephas beckoned, that he should ask him who this *was*, concerning [3] whom he spoke. And that disciple

leaned on Jesus' breast, and said unto him, [4] My Lord, who is this? Jesus answered and said, He to whom I shall dip bread, and give it. And Jesus dipped bread, and gave to Judas, the son of Simon Iscariot. [5] And after the bread, Satan entered him. And Jesus said unto him, What thou [6] desires to do, hasten the doing of it. And no man of them that sat knew why he [7] said this unto him. And some of them thought, because Judas had the box, that he was bidding him buy what would be needed for the feast; or, that he might pay [8] something to the poor. Judas the betrayer answered and said, Can it be I, my [9] Master? Jesus said unto him, Thou hast said. And Judas took the bread straightway, and went forth without: and it was still night.

[10] And Jesus said, Now is the Son of man being glorified, and God is being glorified [11] in him; and if God is glorified in him, God also will glorify him in him, and straightway will glorify him.

[12] And while they were eating, Jesus took bread, and blessed, and divided; and he [13] gave to his disciples, and said unto them, Take and eat; this is my body. And he [Arabic, p. 171] took a cup, and gave thanks, and blessed, and gave them, and said, Take [14, 15] and drink of it, all of you. And they drank of it, all of them. And he said unto them, This is my blood, the new covenant, that is shed for many for the [16] forgiveness of sins. I say unto you, I shall not drink henceforth of this, the juice of the vine, until the day in which I drink with you new *wine* in the kingdom of [17] God. And thus do ye in remembrance of me. And Jesus said unto Simon, Simon, [18] behold, Satan asked that he may sift you like wheat: but I entreat for thee, that thou lose not thy faith:

and do thou, at some time, turn and strengthen thy brethren.

[19] My children, another little *while* am I with you. And ye shall seek me: and as [20] I said unto the Jews, Whither I go, ye cannot come; I say unto you now also. A new commandment I give you, that ye may love one another; and as I have loved [21] you, so shall ye also love one another. By this shall every man know that ye are [22] my disciples, if ye have love one to another. Simon Cephas said unto him, Our Lord, whither goes thou? Jesus answered and said unto him, Whither I go, thou canst not now follow me; but later thou shalt come.

[23] Then said Jesus unto them, Ye all shall desert me this night: it is written, I [24] will smite the shepherd, and the sheep of the flock shall be scattered. But after my [25] rising, I shall go before you into Galilee. Simon Cephas answered and said unto [26] him, My Lord, if every man desert thee, I shall at no time desert thee. I am with thee ready for imprisonment and for death. And my life will I give up for thee. [27] [Arabic, p. 172] Jesus said unto him, Wilt thou give up thy life for me? Verily, verily, I say unto thee, Thou shalt to-day, during this night, before the cock crow [28] twice, three times deny me, that thou knows me not. But Cephas said the more, Even if it lead to death with thee, I shall not deny thee, my Lord. And in like manner said all the disciples also.

[29] Then Jesus said unto them, Let not your hearts be troubled: believe in God, [30] and believe in me. The stations in my Father's house are many, else I should [31] have told you. I go to prepare for you a place. And if I go *to* prepare for you a place, I shall return again, and take you unto me: and so where I am, there ye [32, 33] shall be also. And the place that I go ye know, and the

way ye know. Thomas said unto him, Our Lord, we know not whither thou goes; and how is the way for [34] us to the knowledge of that? Jesus said unto him, I am the way, and the truth, [35] and the life: and no man cometh unto my Father, but through me. And if ye had known me, ye should have known my Father: and from henceforth ye know him, [36] and have seen him. Philip said unto him, Our Lord, shew us the Father, and it suffices [37] us. Jesus said unto him, Have I been all this time with you, and dost thou not know me, Philip? Whosoever hath seen me hath seen the Father; how then says [38] thou, Shew us the Father? Believes thou not that I am in my Father, and my Father in me? And the saying that I say, I say not of myself: but my Father who dwells in [39] me, he doeth these deeds. Believe that I am in my Father, and my Father in me: [40] [Arabic, p. 173] or else believe for the sake of the deeds. Verily, verily, I say unto you, Whosoever believeth in me, the deeds that I do shall he do also; and [41] more than that shall he do: I go unto the Father. And what ye shall ask in my [42] name, I shall do unto you, that the Father may be glorified in his Son. And if ye [43, 44] ask me in my name, I will do *it*. If ye love me, keep my commandments. And I will entreat of my Father, and he will send unto you another Paraclete, that he [45] may be with you forever, *even* the Spirit of truth: whom the world cannot receive; for it hath not seen him, nor known him: but ye know him; for he hath dwelt [46] with you, and is in you. I will not leave you orphans: I will come unto you. [47] Another little *while*, and the world sees me not; but ye see me that I live, and ye [48] shall live also. And in that day ye shall know that I am in my Father, and ye in me, and I in you.

Section XLVI.

[1] Whosoever hath my commandments, and kept them, he it is that loves me: and he that loves me shall be loved of my Father, and I will love him, and will [2] shew myself unto him. Judas (not Iscariot) said unto him, My Lord, what is the [3] purpose of thy intention to shew thyself to us, and not to the world? Jesus answered and said unto him, Whosoever loves me will keep my word: and my Father will love him, and to him will we come, and make our abode with him. [4] But he that loves me not kept not my word: and this word that ye hear is not my word, but the Father's which sent me.

[5, 6] This have I spoken unto you, while I was yet with you. But the Paraclete, the Holy Spirit, whom my Father will send in my name, he will teach you everything, and [7] [Arabic, p. 174] he will bring to your remembrance all that I say unto you. Peace I leave you; my peace I give unto you: and not as this world giveth, give I unto you. [8] Let your heart not be troubled, nor fearful. Ye heard that I said unto you, that I go away, and come unto you. If ye loved me, ye would rejoice, that I go away to my [9] Father: for my Father is greater than I. And now I say unto you before it come [10] to pass, that, when it cometh to pass, ye may believe me. Now I will not speak with you much: the Archon of the world will come, and he will have nothing in [11] me: but that the world may know that I love my Father, and as my Father charged me, so I do.

[12] And he said unto them, When I sent you without purses, or wallets, and shoes, [13] lacked ye perchance anything? They said unto him, Nothing. He said unto them, Henceforth, whosoever hath a purse, let him take it, and likewise the wallet also: and whosoever

hath not a sword, shall sell his garment, and buy for himself a [14] sword. I say unto you, that this scripture also must be fulfilled in me, that I should be reckoned with the transgressors: for all that is said of me is fulfilled in [15] me. His disciples said unto him, Our Lord, lo, here are two swords. He said [16] unto them, They are sufficient. Arise, let us go hence. And they arose, and praised, and went forth, and went, according to their custom, to the Mount of Olives, he and his disciples.

[17] And he said unto them, I am the true vine, and my Father is the husbandman. [18] Every branch that produces not fruit in me, he takes it: and that which gives fruit, [19] he cleanses it, that it may give much fruit. Ye are already clean because of the word [20] that I have spoken unto you. Abide in me, and I in you. And as the branch of the [Arabic, p. 175] vine cannot produce fruit of itself, if it be not abiding in the vine; so too ye [21] also, if ye abide not in me. 3190I am the vine, and ye are the branches: He then that abides in me, and I in him, he giveth much fruit: for without me ye cannot [22] do anything. And if a man abide not in me, he is cast without, like a withered [23] branch; and it is gathered, and cast into the fire, that it may be burned. If ye abide in me, and my word abide in you, everything that ye desire to ask shall be [24] *done* unto you. And herein is the Father glorified, that ye may give much fruit; [25] and ye *shall* be my disciples. And as my Father loved me, I loved you also: [26] abide in my love. If ye keep my commands, ye shall abide in my love; as I have [27] kept my Father's commands, and abode in his love. I have spoken that unto you, [28] that my joy may be in you, and your joy be fulfilled. This is my commandment, [29] that ye love one another, as I loved you. And no love is greater than this,

namely, [30] that a man should give his life for his friends. Ye are my friends, if ye do all that [31] I command you. I call you not now servants; for the servant knows not what his lord doeth: my friends have I now called you; for everything that I heard from [32] my Father I have made known unto you. Ye did not choose me, but I chose I you, and appointed you, that ye also should go and bear fruit, and *that* your fruit should [33] abide; and *that* all that ye shall ask my Father in my name, he may give you. This [34] I command you, that ye love one another. And if the world hate you, know that [35] before you it hated me. If then ye were of the world, the world would love its own: but ye are not of the world: I chose you out of the world: therefore the world [36] [Arabic, p. 176] hated you. Remember the word that I said unto you, that no servant is greater than his lord. And if they persecuted me, you also will they [37] persecute; and if they kept my word, your word also will they keep. But all these things will they do unto you for my name's sake, for they have not known him [38] that sent me. And if I had not come and spoken unto them, they had not had sin: [39] but now they have no excuse for their sins. Whosoever hated me, also hated my [40] Father. And if I had not done the deeds before them that no other man did, they would not have had sin: but now they have seen and hated me and my Father [41] also: that the word may be fulfilled that is written in their law, They hated me for [42] nothing. But when the Paraclete is come, whom I will send unto you from my Father, even the Spirit of truth, which goes forth from my Father, he shall bear witness of [43] me: and ye also bear witness, because from the beginning ye *have been* with me.

[44, 45] I have said that unto you, that ye may not stumble. And they shall put you out of their synagogues: and there comes an hour when everyone that kills [46] you shall think that he hath offered unto God an offering. And they will do that, [47] because they do not know me, nor my Father. I have said that unto you, so that [48] when its time is come, ye may remember it, that I told you. And this hitherto I said not unto you, because I was with you. But now I go unto him that sent me; and no [49] man of you asked me whither I go. I have said that unto you now, and grief hath [50] come and taken possession of your hearts But I say the truth unto you; It is better for you that I go away: for if I go not away, the Paraclete will not come unto you; [51] [Arabic, p. 177] but if I go away, I will send him unto you. And when he cometh, he will reprove the world for sin, and for righteousness, and for judgement: [52, 53] for sin, because they have not believed in me; and for righteousness, because I go [54] to my Father; and for judgement, because the Archon of this world hath been [55] judged. And further have I many things to speak unto you, but ye cannot tarry [56] now. Howbeit when the Spirit of truth is come, he will remind you of all the truth: he will say nothing from himself; but everything that he hears, that shall [57] he say: and he shall make known unto you the things that are to be. And he shall [58] glorify me; for from me shall he take and shew you. All that my Father hath is mine: therefore said I unto you, that he taketh of mine, and shall shew you.

Section XLVII.
[1] A little *while*, and ye shall not behold me; and a little *while* again, and ye shall [2] behold me; because I

go to the Father. His disciples therefore said one to another, What is this that he hath said unto us, A little *while*, and ye shall not behold me; and a little *while* again, and ye shall behold me: and, I go to my [3] Father? And they said, What is this little *while* that he hath said? We know not [4] what he speaks. And Jesus perceived that they were seeking to ask him, and said unto them, Do ye inquire among yourselves concerning this, that I said unto you, A little *while*, and ye behold me not, and a little while again, and ye shall [5] behold me? Verily, verily, I say unto you, that ye shall weep and grieve, but the world shall rejoice: and ye shall be sorrowful, but your grief shall turn to joy.

[6] For, a woman when the time is come for her that she should bring forth, the arrival of the day of her bringing forth distressed her: but whenever she hath brought forth a son, she remembered not her distress, for joy at the birth of a man into the [7] world. And ye now also grieve: but I shall see you, and your hearts shall rejoice, [8] [Arabic, p. 178] and your joy no man taketh from you. And in that day ye shall ask me nothing. And verily, verily, I say unto you, All that ye ask my Father in my name, he will give you. Hitherto ye have asked nothing [9] in my name: ask, and ye shall receive, that your joy may be complete.

[10] I have spoken unto you now in ænigmas: but there will come an hour when I shall not speak to you in ænigmas, but shall reveal unto you the Father plainly, [11] in that day when ye shall ask in my name: and I say not unto you, that I shall [12] entreat the Father for you; for the Father loves you, because ye have loved me, [13] and have believed that I came forth from my Father. I came forth from my Father, and came into the world: and

I leave the world, and go unto my Father. [14] His disciples said unto him, Lo, thy speech is now plain, and thou hast not said one [15] thing in an ænigma. Now, lo, we know that thou knows everything, and needs not that any man should ask thee: and by this we believe that thou comes forth [16, 17] from God. Jesus said unto them, Believe that an hour cometh, and lo, it hath come, and ye shall be scattered, every one of you to his place, and shall leave me [18] alone: and yet I am not alone, because the Father is with me. This have I said unto you, that in me ye may have peace. And in the world trouble shall overtake you: but be of good courage; for I have overcome the world.

[19] This said Jesus, and lifted up his eyes unto heaven, and said, My Father, the hour [20] is come; glorify thy Son, that thy Son may glorify thee: as thou gives him authority [21] over all flesh, that all that thou hast given him, he might give them eternal life. And this is eternal life, that they should know that thou alone art true God, and *that he* [22] [Arabic, p. 179] whom thou didst send is Jesus the Messiah. I glorified thee in the earth, [23] and the work which thou gives me to do I have accomplished. And now glorify thou me, O Father, beside thee, with that glory which I had with thee [24] before the world was. I made known thy name to the men whom thou gives me out of the world: thine they were, and thou gives them to me; and they have kept [25, 26] thy word. Now they know that all that thou hast given me is from thee: and the sayings which thou gives me I have given unto them; and they received *them*, and knew of a truth that I came forth from thee, and believed that thou didst send me. [27] And I ask for their sake: and my asking is not for the world, but for those whom [28] thou hast given

me; for they are thine: and all that is mine is thine, and all that is [29] thine is mine: and I am glorified in them. And now I am not in the world, and they are in the world, and I come to thee. My holy Father, keep them in thy [30] name which thou hast given unto me, that they may be one, as we are. When I was with them in the world, I kept them in thy name: and I kept those whom thou gives unto me: and no man of them hath perished, but the son of perdition; that [31] the scripture might be fulfilled. Now I come to thee: and this I say in the world, [32] that my joy may be complete in them. I have given them thy word; and the world [33] hated them, because they were not of the world, as I was not of the world. And I ask not this, that thou take them from the world, but that thou keep them from the [34, 35] evil one. They were not of the world, as I was not of the world. O Father, sanctify [36] them in thy truth: for thy word is truth. And as thou didst send me into the world, I [37] [Arabic, p. 180] also send them into the world. And for their sake I sanctify myself, that they [38] also may be sanctified in the truth. Neither for these alone do I ask, but for [39] the sake of them that believe in me through their word; that they may be all one; as thou art in me, and I in thee, and so they also shall be one in us: that the world [40] may believe that thou didst send me. And the glory which thou hast given unto [41] me I have given unto them; that they may be one, as we are one; I in them, and thou in me, that they may be perfect into one; and *that* the world may know that [42] thou didst send me, and that I loved them, as thou loves me. Father, and those whom thou hast given me, I wish that, where I am, they may be with me also; that they may behold my glory, which thou hast given me: for thou loves me before [43] the foundation of the world. My righteous Father, and the world knew thee not, [44] but I know thee; and they knew that thou didst send me; and I made known unto them thy name, and will make it known to them; that the love *wherewith* thou loves me may be in them, and I shall be in them.

Section XLVIII.

[1] This said Jesus, and went forth with his disciples to a place which was called Gethsemane, on the side that is in the plain of Kidron, the mountain, the place [2] in which was a garden; and he entered thither, he and his disciples. And Judas the [3] betrayer knew that place: for Jesus oft-times met with his disciples there. And when Jesus came to the place, he said to his disciples, Sit ye here, so that I may go and pray; [4, 5] [Arabic, p. 181] and pray ye, that ye enter not into temptations. And he took with him Cephas and the sons of Zebedee together, James and John; and he began to [6] look sorrowful, and to be anxious. And he said unto them, My soul is distressed unto [7] death: abide ye here, and watch with me. And he withdrew from them a little, [8] the space of a stone's throw; and he kneeled, and fell on his face, and prayed, so [9] that, if it *were* possible, this hour *might* pass him. And he said, Father, thou art able for all things; if thou wilt, let this cup pass me: but let not my will be *done*, [10] but let thy will be *done*. And he came to his disciples, and found them sleeping; [11] and he said unto Cephas, Simon, didst thou sleep? Could ye thus not for one hour [12] watch with me? Watch and pray, that ye enter not into temptations: the spirit is [13] willing and ready, but the body is weak. And he went again a second time, and prayed, and said, My Father, if it is not possible with regard to this cup that it pass, [14] except I drink it,

thy will be *done*. And he returned again, and found his disciples sleeping, for their eyes were heavy from their grief and anxiety; and they knew not [15] what to say to him. And he left them, and went away again, and prayed a third [16] time, and said the very same word. And there appeared unto him an angel from [17] heaven, encouraging him. And being afraid he prayed continuously: and his sweat [18] [Arabic, p. 182] became like a stream of blood, and fell on the ground. Then he rose from [19] his prayer, and came to his disciples, and found them sleeping. And he [20] said unto them, Sleep now, and rest: the end hath arrived, and the hour hath come; [21] and behold, the Son of man is betrayed into the hands of sinners. Arise, let us go: for he hath come that betrayed me.

[22] And while he was still speaking, came Judas the betrayer, one of the twelve, and with him a great multitude carrying lanterns and torches and swords and staves, from the chief priests and scribes and elders of the people, and with him the foot soldiers [23] of the Romans. And Judas the betrayer gave them a sign, and said, He whom I shall kiss, he is he: take him with care, and lead him *away*.

[24] And Jesus, because he knew everything that should come upon him, went forth [25] unto them. And immediately Judas the betrayer came to Jesus, and said, Peace, [26] my Master; and kissed him. And Jesus said unto him, Judas, with a kiss betrays [27] thou the Son of man? *Was it* for that thou comes, my friend? And Jesus said [28] to those that came unto him, Whom seek ye? They said unto him, Jesus the Nazarene. Jesus said unto them, I am he. And Judas the betrayer also was standing [29] with them. And when Jesus said unto them, I am he,

they retreated backward, and [30] fell to the ground. And Jesus asked them again, Whom seek ye? They answered, [31] Jesus the Nazarene. Jesus said unto them, I told you that I am he: and if ye seek [32] me, let these go away: that the word might be fulfilled which he spoke, Of those [33] [Arabic, p. 183] whom thou hast given me I lost not even one. Then came those that were with Judas, and seized Jesus, and took him.

[34] And when his disciples saw what happened, they said, Our Lord, shall we smite [35] them with swords? And Simon Cephas had a sword, and he drew it, and struck the servant of the chief priest, and cut off his right ear. And the name of that servant [36] was Malchus. Jesus said unto Cephas, The cup which my Father hath given [37] me, shall I not drink it? Put the sword into its sheath: for all that take with the [38] sword shall die by the sword. Thinks thou that I am not able to ask of my [39] Father, and he shall now raise up for me more than twelve tribes of angels? Then [40] how should the scriptures which were spoken be fulfilled, that thus it must be? Your [41] leave in this. And he touched the ear of him that was struck, and healed it. And in that hour Jesus said to the multitudes, As they come out against a thief are ye come out against me with swords and staves to take me? Daily was I with you in [42] the temple sitting teaching, and ye took me not: but this is your hour, and the power [43] of darkness. And that was, that the scriptures of the prophets might be fulfilled.

[44] Then the disciples all left him, and fled. And the foot soldiers and the officers [45] and the soldiers of the Jews seized Jesus, and came. And a certain young man [46] followed him, and he was wrapped in a towel, naked: and they seized him; so he [47] [Arabic, p. 184]

left the towel, and fled naked. Then they took Jesus, and bound him, and brought him to Annas first; because he was the father in law of Caiaphas, [48] who was chief priest that year. And Caiaphas was he that counselled the Jews, that it was necessary that one man should die instead of the people.

[49] And Simon Cephas and one of the other disciples followed Jesus. And the chief [50] priest knew that disciple, and he entered with Jesus into the court; but Simon was standing without at the door. And that other disciple, whom the chief priest knew, [51] went out and spoke unto her that kept the door, and she brought Simon in. And when the maid that kept the door saw Simon, she looked steadfastly at him, and said unto him, Art not thou also one of the disciples of this man, I mean Jesus the [52] Nazarene? But he denied, and said, Woman, I know him not, neither know I even [53] what thou says. And the servants and the soldiers rose, and made a fire in the [54] middle of the court, that they might warm themselves; for it was cold. And when [55] the fire burned up, they sat down around it. And Simon also came, and sat down with them to warm himself, that he might see the end of what should happen.

Section XLIX.

[1, 2] And the chief priest asked Jesus about his disciples, and about his doctrine. And Jesus said unto him, I was speaking openly to the people; and I ever taught in the synagogue, and in the temple, where all the Jews gather; and I have spoken nothing in [3] [Arabic, p. 185] secret. Why asks thou me? Ask those that have heard, what I spoke unto [4] them: for they know all that I said. And when he had said that, one of the soldiers which were

standing *there* struck the cheek of Jesus, and said unto him, [5] Do you thus answer the chief priest? Jesus answered and said unto him, If I [6] have spoken evil, bear witness of evil: but if well, why did you smite me? And Annas sent Jesus bound unto Caiaphas the chief priest.

[7] And when Jesus went out, Simon Cephas was standing in the outer court warming [8] himself. And that maid saw him again, and began to say to those that stood [9] *by*, This *man* also was there with Jesus the Nazarene. And those that stood *by* [10] came forward and said to Cephas, Truly thou art one of his disciples. And he [11] denied again with an oath, I know not the man. And after a little one of the servants of the chief priest, the kinsman of him whose ear Simon cut off, saw him; and [12] he disputed and said, Truly this *man* was with him: and he also is a Galilæan; [13] and his speech resembles. And he said unto Simon, Did not I see thee with him [14] in the garden? Then began Simon to curse, and to swear, I know not this man [15] whom ye have mentioned. And immediately, while he was speaking, the cock crew [16] twice. And in that hour Jesus turned, he being without, and looked steadfastly at Cephas. And Simon remembered the word of our Lord, which he said unto him, [17, 18] Before the cock crow twice, thou shalt deny me thrice. And Simon went forth without, and wept bitterly.

[19] [Arabic, p. 186] And when the morning approached, the servants of all the chief priests and the scribes and the elders of the people and all the multitude assembled, [20, 21] and made a plot; and they took counsel against Jesus to put him to death. And they sought false witnesses who should witness against him,

that they might put him to [22, 23] death, and they found not; but many false witnesses came, but their witness did not [24, 25] agree. But at last there came two lying witnesses, and said, We heard him say, I will destroy this temple of God that is made with hands, and will build another not [26, 27] made with hands after three days. And not even so did their witness agree. But Jesus was silent. And the chief priest rose in the midst, and asked Jesus, and said, [28] Answers thou not a word concerning anything? What do these witness against [29, 30] thee? But Jesus was silent, and answered him nothing. And they took him up [31] into their assembly, and said unto him, If thou art the Messiah, tell us. He said [32] unto them, If I tell you, ye will not believe me: and if I ask you, ye will not answer [33] me a word, nor let me go. And the chief priest answered and said unto him, I adjure thee by the living God, that thou tell us whether thou art the Messiah, the [34, 35] Son of the living God. Jesus said unto him, Thou hast said that I am he. They all said unto him, Then thou art now the Son of God? Jesus said, Ye have said [36] that I am he. I say unto you, that henceforth ye shall see the Son of man sitting [37] [Arabic, p. 187] at the right hand of power, and coming on the clouds of heaven. Then the [38] chief priest rent his tunic, and said, He hath blasphemed. And they all said, Why should we seek now witnesses? We have heard now the blasphemy from his mouth. [39, 40] What then think ye? They all answered and said, He is worthy of death. Then some of them drew near, and spat in his face, and struck him, and scoffed at him. [41] And the soldiers struck him on his cheeks, and said, Prophesy unto us, *thou* Messiah: [42] who is he that struck thee? And many other things spoke they falsely, and said against him.

[43] And all of their assembly arose, and took Jesus, and brought him bound to [44] the prætorium, and delivered him up to Pilate the judge; but they entered not into the prætorium, that they might not be defiled when they should eat the Passover.

[45] And Jesus stood before the judge. And Pilate went forth unto them without, and [46] said unto them, What accusation have ye against this man? They answered and said unto him, If he had not been doing evils, neither should we have delivered [47] him up unto thee. We found this *man* leading our people astray, and restraining from giving tribute to Cæsar, and saying of himself that he is the King, the Messiah. [48] Pilate said unto them, Then take ye him, and judge him according to your law. [Arabic, p.188] The Jews said unto him, We have no authority to put a man to death: [49] that the word might be fulfilled, which Jesus spoke, when he made known by what manner of death he was to die.

[50] And Pilate entered into the prætorium, and called Jesus, and said unto him, Art [51] thou the King of the Jews? Jesus said unto him, Of thyself said thou this, or [52] did others tell it thee concerning me? Pilate said unto him, Am I, forsooth, a Jew? The sons of thy nation and the chief priests delivered thee unto me: what [53] hast thou done? Jesus said unto him, My kingdom is not of this world: if my kingdom were of this world, then would my servants fight, that I should not be [54] delivered to the Jews: now my kingdom is not from hence. Pilate said unto him, Then *thou art* a king? Jesus said unto him, Thou hast said that I am a king. And for this was I born, and for this came I into the world, that I should bear witness [55] of the truth. And every one that is of the truth

hears my voice. Pilate said unto him, And what is the truth? And when he said that, he went out again unto the Jews.

Section L.

[1] And Pilate said unto the chief priests and the multitude, I have not found [2] against this man anything. But they cried out and said, He hath disquieted our people with his teaching in all Judæa, and he began from Galilee and unto this [3] place. And Pilate, when he heard the name of Galilee, asked, Is this man a Galilæan? [4] And when he learned that he was under the jurisdiction of Herod, he sent him to Herod: for he was in Jerusalem in those days.

[5] And Herod, when he saw Jesus, rejoiced exceedingly: for he had desired to see him for a long time, because he had heard regarding him many things; and he counted on [6] [Arabic, p. 189] seeing some sign from him. And he questioned him with many words; but [7] Jesus answered him not a word. And the scribes and chief priests were [8] standing *by*, and they accused him vehemently. And Herod scoffed at him, he and his servants; and when he had scoffed at him, he clothed him in robes of scarlet, [9] and sent him to Pilate. And on that day Pilate and Herod became friends, there having been enmity between them before that.

[10, 11] And Pilate called the chief priests and the rulers of the people, and said unto them, Ye brought unto me this man, as the perverter of your people: and I have tried him before you, and have not found in this man any cause of all that ye [12] seek against him: nor yet Herod: for I sent him unto him; and he hath done [13] nothing for which he should deserve death. So now I will chastise

him, and let [14, 15] him go. The multitude all cried out and said, Take him from us, take him. And [16] the chief priests and the elders accused him of many things. And during their [17] accusation he answered not a word. Then Pilate said unto him, Hears thou not [18] how many *things* they witness against thee? And he answered him not, not even one word: and Pilate marveled at that.

[19] And when the judge sat on his tribune, his wife sent unto him, and said unto him, See that thou have nothing to do with that righteous *man*: for I have suffered much in my dream to-day because of him.

[20] And at every feast the custom of the judge was to release to the people one [21] prisoner, him whom they would. And there was in their prison a well-known prisoner, [22, 23] called Barabbas. And when they assembled, Pilate said unto them, Ye have a custom, that I should release unto you a prisoner at the Passover: will ye that I [24] release unto you the King of the Jews? And they all cried out and said, Release not [Arabic, p. 190] unto us this *man*, but release unto us Barabbas. And this Barabbas was a [25] robber, who for sedition and murder, which was in the city, was cast into the [26] prison. And all the people cried out and began to ask *him to do* as the custom was [27] that he should do with them. And Pilate answered and said unto them, Whom will ye that I release unto you? Barabbas, or Jesus which is called the Messiah, the [28] King of the Jews? For Pilate knew that envy had moved them to deliver him up. [29] And the chief priests and the elders asked the multitudes to deliver Barabbas, and [30] to destroy Jesus. The judge answered and said unto them, Whom of the two will [31] ye that I release unto you? They said, Barabbas. Pilate said unto them, And [32] Jesus which is called the Messiah, what shall I

do with him? They all cried out [33] and said, Crucify him. And Pilate spoke to them again, for he desired to release [34] Jesus; but they cried out and said, Crucify him, crucify him, and release unto us [35] Barabbas. And Pilate said unto them a third time, What evil hath this *man* done? I have not found in him any cause to necessitate death: I will chastise him and [36] let him go. But they increased in importunity with a loud voice, and asked him to crucify him. And their voice, and the voice of the chief priests, prevailed. [37] Then Pilate released unto them that one who was cast into prison for sedition and murder, Barabbas, whom they asked for: and he scourged Jesus with whips.

[38] Then the foot soldiers of the judge took Jesus, and went into the prætorium, and [39] [Arabic, p. 191] gathered unto him all of the foot soldiers. And they stripped him, and put on [40] him a scarlet cloak. And they clothed him in garments of purple, and plaited [41] a crown of thorns, and placed it on his head, and a reed in his right hand; and while they mocked at him and laughed, they fell down on their knees before him, and bowed [42] down to him, and said, Hail, King of the Jews! And they spat in his face, and took the reed from his hand, and struck him on his head, and smote his cheeks. [43] And Pilate went forth without again, and said unto the Jews, I bring him forth to [44] you, that ye may know that I do not find, in examining him, even one crime. And Jesus went forth without, wearing the crown of thorns and the purple garments. [45] Pilate said unto them, Behold, the man! And when the chief priests and the soldiers saw him, they cried out and said, Crucify him, crucify him. Pilate said unto them, Take him yourselves, and crucify him: for I find not a cause against [46] him.

The Jews said unto him, We have a law, and according to our law he deserves [47] death, because he made himself the Son of God. And when Pilate heard this word, [48] his fear increased; and he entered again into the porch, and said to Jesus, Whence [49] art thou? But Jesus answered him not a word. Pilate said unto him, Speaks thou not unto me? Knows thou not that I have authority to release thee, and have [50] authority to crucify thee? Jesus said unto him, Thou hast not any authority over me, if thou wert not given *it* from above: therefore the sin of him that delivered [51] me up unto thee is greater than thy sin. And for this word Pilate wished to release him: but the Jews cried out, If thou let him go, thou art not a friend of Cæsar: for everyone that makes himself a king is against Cæsar.

Section LI.

[1] [Arabic, p. 192] And when Pilate heard this saying, he took Jesus out, and sat on the tribune in the place which was called the pavement of stones, but in the Hebrew [2] called Gabbatha. And that day was the Friday of the Passover: and it had reached [3] about the sixth hour. And he said to the Jews, Behold, your King! And they cried out, Take him, take him, crucify him, crucify him. Pilate said unto them, Shall I crucify your King? The chief priests said unto him, We have no king except [4] Cæsar. And Pilate, when he saw *it*, and he was gaining nothing, but the tumult was increasing, took water, and washed his hands before the multitude, and said, I [5] am innocent of the blood of this innocent *man*: ye shall know. And all the people [6] answered and said, His blood be on us, and on our children. Then Pilate commanded to grant

them their request; and delivered up Jesus to be crucified, according to their wish.

[7] Then Judas the betrayer, when he saw Jesus wronged, went and returned the [8] thirty *pieces* of money to the chief priests and the elders, and said, I have sinned in my betraying innocent blood. And they said unto him, And we, what must we *do*? [9] Know thou. And he threw down the money in the temple, and departed; and *he* [10] went away and hanged himself. And the chief priests took the money, and said, We have not authority to cast it into the place of the offering, for it is the price [11] of blood. And they took counsel, and bought with it the plain of the potter, for [12] the burial of strangers. Therefore that plain was called, The field of blood, unto [13] [Arabic, p. 193] this day. Therein was fulfilled the saying in the prophet which said, I took thirty *pieces* of money, the price of the precious *one, which was* fixed [14] by the children of Israel; and I paid them for the plain of the potter, as the Lord commanded me.

[15] And the Jews took Jesus, and went away to crucify him. And when he bare his [16] cross and went out, they stripped him of those purple and scarlet garments which he [17] had on, and put on him his *own* garments. And while they were going with him, they found a man, a Cyrenian, coming from the country, named Simon, the father of Alexander and Rufus: and they compelled this *man* to bear the cross of Jesus. [18] And they took the cross and laid it upon him, that he might bear it, and come after Jesus; and Jesus went, and his cross behind him.

[19] And there followed him much people, and women which were lamenting and [20] raving. But Jesus turned unto them and said, Daughters of Jerusalem, weep

not [21] for me: weep for yourselves, and for your children. Days are coming, when they shall say, Blessed are the barren, and the wombs that bare not, and the breasts [22] that gave not suck. Then shall they begin to say to the mountains, Fall on us; and [23] to the hills, Cover us. For if they do so in the green tree, what shall be in the dry?

[24] And they brought with Jesus two others of the malefactors, to be put to death.

[25] And when they came unto a certain place called The skull, and called in the Hebrew Golgotha, they crucified him there: they crucified with him these two [26] malefactors, one on his right, and the other on his left. And the scripture was [27] [Arabic, p. 194] fulfilled, which said, He was numbered with the transgressors. And they gave him to drink wine and myrrh, and vinegar which had been mixed with the myrrh; and he tasted, and would not drink; and he received it not.

[28] And the soldiers, when they had crucified Jesus, took his garments, and cast lots for them in four parts, to every party of the soldiers a part; and his tunic was [29] without sewing, from the top woven throughout. And they said one to another, Let us not rend it, but cast lots for it, whose it shall be: and the scripture was fulfilled, which said,

They divided my garments among them,
And cast the lot for my vesture.

[30, 31] This the soldiers did. And they sat and guarded him there. And Pilate wrote on a tablet the cause of his death, and put it on the wood of the cross above his head. And there was written upon it thus: This is Jesus the Nazarene, the King of the [32] Jews. And this tablet read many of the Jews: for the place where Jesus was crucified

was near the city: and it was written in Hebrew and Greek and Latin. [33] And the chief priests said unto Pilate, Write not, The King of the Jews; but, He it is [34] that said, I am the King of the Jews. Pilate said unto them, What hath been [35] written hath been written. And the people were standing beholding; and they [36] that passed by were reviling him, and shaking their heads, and saying, Thou that destroys the temple, and builds it in three days, save thyself if thou art the Son [37] of God, and come down from the cross. And in like manner the chief priests and the [Arabic, p. 195] scribes and the elders and the Pharisees derided him, and laughed one with [38, 39] another, and said, The savior of others cannot save himself. If he is the Messiah, the chosen of God, and the King of Israel, let him come down now from the [40] cross, that we may see, and believe in him. He that relies on God—let him deliver him [41] now, if he is pleased with him: for he said, I am the Son of God. And the soldiers [42] also scoffed at him in that they came near unto him, and brought him vinegar, and [43] said unto him, If thou art the King of the Jews, save thyself. And likewise the two robbers also that were crucified with him reproached him.

[44] And one of those two malefactors who were crucified with him reviled him, and [45] said, If thou art the Messiah, save thyself, and save us also. But his comrade rebuked him, and said, Does thou not even fear God, being thyself also in this [46] condemnation? And we with justice, and as we deserved, and according to our deed, have we been rewarded: but this *man* hath not done anything unlawful. [47] And he said unto Jesus, Remember me, my Lord, when thou comes in thy

kingdom. [48] Jesus said unto him, Verily I say unto thee, To-day shalt thou be with me in Paradise.

[49] And there stood by the cross of Jesus his mother, and his mother's sister, [50] Mary that was related to Clopas, and Mary Magdalene. And Jesus saw his mother, and that disciple whom he loved standing *by*; and he said to his mother, [51] Woman, behold, thy son! And he said to that disciple, Behold, thy mother! And from that hour that disciple took her unto him*self*.

[52] [Arabic, p. 196] And from the sixth hour darkness was on all the land unto the ninth [53] hour, and the sun became dark. And at the ninth hour Jesus cried out with a loud voice, and said, Yail, Yaili, why hast thou forsaken me? Which is, My [54] God, my God, why hast thou forsaken me? And some of those that stood there, when they heard, said, This *man* called Elijah.

Section LII.
[1] And after that, Jesus knew that all things were finished; and that the scripture [2] might be accomplished, he said, I thirst. And there was set a vessel full of vinegar: and in that hour one of them hasted, and took a sponge, and filled it with that [3] vinegar, and fastened it on a reed, and brought it near his mouth to give him a [4] drink. And when Jesus had taken that vinegar, he said, Everything is finished. [5] But the rest said, Let be, that we may see whether Elijah cometh to save him. [6, 7] And Jesus said, My Father, forgive them; for they know not what they do. And Jesus cried again with a loud voice, and said, My Father, into thy hands I commend3626 my spirit. He said that, and bowed his head, and gave up his spirit.

[8] And immediately the face of the door of the temple was rent into two parts from [9] top to bottom; and the earth was shaken; and the stones were split to pieces; and the [Arabic, p. 197] tombs were opened; and the bodies of many saints which slept, arose and [10] came forth; and after his resurrection they entered into the holy city and [11] appeared unto many. And the officer of the foot soldiers, and they that were with him who were guarding Jesus, when they saw the earthquake, and the things which came [12] to pass, feared greatly, and praised God, and said, This man *was* righteous; and, [13] Truly he was the Son of God. And all the multitudes that were come together to the sight, when they saw what came to pass, returned and smote upon their breasts.

[14] And the Jews, because of the Friday, said, Let these bodies not remain on their crosses, because it is the morning of the Sabbath (for that Sabbath was a great day); and they asked of Pilate that they might break the legs of those that were [15] crucified, and take them down. And the soldiers came, and brake the legs of the [16] first, and that other which was crucified with him: but when they came to Jesus, [17] they saw that he had died before, so they brake not his legs: 3640but one of the soldiers pierced him in his side with a spear, and immediately there came forth blood and [18] water. And he that hath seen hath borne witness, and his witness is true: and he [19] knows that he hath said the truth, that ye also may believe. This he did, that [20] the scripture might be fulfilled, which said, A bone shall not be broken in him; and the scripture also which said, Let them look upon him whom they pierced.

[21] And there were in the distance all the acquaintance of Jesus standing, and the women that came

with him from Galilee, those that followed him and ministered. [22] One of them was Mary Magdalene; and Mary the mother of James the little and [23] [Arabic, p. 198] Joses, and the mother of the sons of Zebedee, and Salome, and many others which came up with him unto Jerusalem; and they saw that.

[24] And when the evening of the Friday was come, because of the entering of the [25] Sabbath, there came a rich man, a noble of Ramah, a city of Judah, named Joseph, and he was a good man and upright; and he was a disciple of Jesus, but [26] was concealing himself for fear of the Jews. And he did not agree with the accusers [27] in their desire and their deeds: and he was looking for the kingdom of God. And this man went boldly, and entered in unto Pilate, and asked of him the body of [28] Jesus. And Pilate wondered how he had died already: and he called the officer of [29] the foot soldiers, and asked him concerning his death before the time. And when [30] he knew, he commanded him to deliver up his body unto Joseph. And Joseph bought for him a winding cloth of pure linen, and took down the body of Jesus, [31] and wound it in it; and they came and took it. And there came unto him Nicodemus also, who of old came unto Jesus by night; and he brought with him perfume [32] of myrrh and aloes, about a hundred pounds. And they took the body of Jesus, and wound it in the linen and the perfume, as was the custom of the Jews to bury.

[33] And there was in the place where Jesus was crucified a garden; and in that garden [34] a new tomb cut out in a rock, wherein was never man yet laid. And they left [35] Jesus there because the Sabbath had come in, and because the tomb was near. And they pushed a great stone, and thrust it against the door of the sepulcher, and

[36] went away. And Mary Magdalene and Mary that was related to Joses came to [37] [Arabic, p. 199] the sepulcher after them, and sat opposite the sepulcher, and saw the [38] body, how they took it in and laid it there. And they returned, and bought ointment and perfume, and prepared *it*, that they might come and anoint him. [39] And on the day which was the Sabbath day they desisted according to the command.

[40, 41] And the chief priests and the Pharisees gathered unto Pilate, and said unto him, Our lord, we remember that that misleader said, while he was alive, After three days [42] I rise. And now send beforehand and guard the tomb until the third day, lest his disciples come and steal him by night, and they will say unto the people that he [43] is risen from the dead: and the last error shall be worse than the first. He said unto them, And have ye not guards? Go, and take precautions as ye know *how*. [44] And they went, and set *guards* at the tomb, and sealed that stone, with the guards.

[45] And in the evening of the Sabbath, which is the morning of the first *day*, and in [46] the dawning while the darkness yet remained, came Mary Magdalene and the other Mary and other women to see the tomb. They brought with them the [47] perfume which they had prepared, and said among themselves, Who is it that will [48] remove for us the stone from the door of the tomb? For it was very great. And when they said thus, there occurred a great earthquake; and an angel came down [49] from heaven, and came and removed the stone from the door. And they came and found the stone removed from the sepulcher, and the angel sitting upon the [50] stone. And his appearance was as the lightning, and his raiment white as the [51] snow: and for fear of him the

The Diatessaron of Tatian

guards were troubled, and became as dead *men*. [52] And when he went away, the women entered into the sepulcher; and they found [53] [Arabic, p. 200] not the body of Jesus. And they saw there a young man sitting on the [54] right, arrayed in a white garment; and they were amazed. And the angel answered and said unto the women, Fear ye not: for I know that ye seek Jesus the [55] Nazarene, who hath been crucified. He is not here; but he is risen, as he said. Come and see the place where our Lord lay.

Section LIII.

[1] And while they marveled at that, behold, two men standing above them, their [2] raiment shining: and they were seized with fright, and bowed down their face to [3] the earth: and they said unto them, Why seek ye the living *one* with the dead? He is not here; he is risen: remember what he was speaking unto you while he was in [4] Galilee, and saying, The Son of man is to be delivered up into the hands of sinners, [5] and to be crucified, and on the third day to rise. But go in haste, and say to his disciples and to Cephas, He is risen from among the dead; and lo, he goes before [6] you into Galilee; and there ye shall see him, where he said unto you: lo, I have [7] told you. And they remembered his sayings; and they departed in haste from the [8] tomb with joy and great fear, and hastened and went; and perplexity and fear [9] encompassed them; and they told no man anything, for they were afraid. And Mary hastened, and came to Simon Cephas, and to that other disciple whom Jesus loved, and said unto them, They have taken our Lord from the sepulcher, and I [10] know not where they have laid him. And Simon went out, and that other disciple, [11] and

came to the sepulcher. And they hastened both together: and that disciple [12] outran Simon, and came first to the sepulcher; and he looked down, and saw the [13] linen laid; but he went not in. And Simon came after him, and entered into the [14] [Arabic, p. 201] sepulcher, and saw the linen laid; and the scarf with which his head was bound was not with the linen, but wrapped and laid aside in a certain place. [15] Then entered that disciple which came first to the sepulcher, and saw, and believed. [16] And they knew not yet from the scriptures that the Messiah was to rise from among [17] the dead. And those two disciples went to their place.

[18] But Mary remained at the tomb weeping: and while she wept, she looked [19] down into the tomb; and she saw two angels sitting in white raiment, one of them toward his pillow, and the other toward his feet, where the body of Jesus had been [20] laid. And they said unto her, Woman, why do you weep? She said unto them, [21] They have taken my Lord, and I know not where they have left him. She said that, and turned behind her, and saw Jesus standing, and knew not that it was [22] Jesus. Jesus said unto her, Woman, why do you weep? Whom do you seek? And she supposed him *to be* the gardener, and said, My lord, if thou hast taken him, [23] tell me where you have laid him, that I may go and take him. Jesus said unto her, Mary. She turned, and said unto him in Hebrew, Rabboni; which is, being [24] interpreted, Teacher. Jesus said unto her, Touch me not; for I have not ascended yet unto my Father: go to my brethren, and say unto them, I ascend unto my Father and your Father, and my God and your God.

[25] And on the First-day on which he rose, he appeared first unto Mary Magdalene, from whom he had cast out seven demons.

[26] And some of those guards came to the city, and informed the chief priests of [27] [Arabic, p. 202] all that had happened. And they assembled with the elders, and took [28] counsel; and they gave money, not a little, to the guards, and said unto them, Say ye, His disciples came and stole him by night, while we were sleeping.

[29] And if the judge hear that, we will make a plea with him, and free you of blame. [30] And they, when they took the money, did according to what they taught them. And this word spread among the Jews unto this day.

[31] And then came Mary Magdalene, and announced to the disciples that she had seen our Lord, and that he had said that unto her.

[32] And while the first women were going in the way to inform his disciples, [33] Jesus met them, and said unto them, Peace unto you. And they came and took [34] hold of his feet, and worshipped him. Then said Jesus unto them, Fear not: but go and say to my brethren that they depart into Galilee, and there they shall see [35] me. And those women returned, and told all that to the eleven, and to the rest of the disciples; and to those that had been with him, for they were saddened and [36] weeping. And those were Mary Magdalene, and Joanna, and Mary the mother of James, and the rest who were with them: and they were those that told the apostles. [37] And they, when they heard them say that he was alive and had appeared unto them, [38] did not believe them: and these sayings were before their eyes as the sayings of madness. [39] [Arabic, p. 203] And after that, he appeared to two of

them, on that day, and while they were going to the village which was named Emmaus, and whose distance [40] from Jerusalem was sixty furlongs. And they were talking the one of them with the [41] other of all the things which had happened. And during the time of their talking and [42] inquiring with one another, Jesus came and reached them, and walked with them. But [43] their eyes were veiled that they should not know him. And he said unto them, What are these sayings which ye address the one of you to the other, as ye walk and are [44] sad? One of them, whose name was Cleopas, answered and said unto him, Art thou perchance alone a stranger to Jerusalem, since thou knows not what was in [45] it in these days? He said unto them, What was? They said unto him, Concerning Jesus, he who was from Nazareth, a man who was a prophet, and powerful in [46] speech and deeds before God and before all the people: and the chief priests and [47] the elders delivered him up to the sentence of death, and crucified him. But we supposed that he was the one who was to deliver Israel. And since all these [48] things happened there have passed three days. But *certain* women of us also [49] informed us that they had come to the sepulcher; and when they found not his body, they came and told us that they had seen there the angels, and they said [50] concerning him that he was alive. And some of us also went to the sepulcher, and [51] found the matter as the women had said: only they saw him not. Then said Jesus [52] unto them, Ye lacking in discernment, and heavy in heart to believe! Was it not in all the sayings of the prophets that the Messiah was to suffer these things, and to [53] [Arabic, p. 204] enter into his Glory? And he began from Moses and from all the prophets, [54] and interpreted to them concerning himself from all the scriptures. And they drew near unto the village, whither they were going: and he was leading them to [55] imagine that he was as if going to a distant region. And they pressed him, and said unto him, Abide with us: for the day hath declined now to the darkness. And he went [56] in to abide with them. And when he sat with them, he took bread, and blessed,[57] and brake, and gave to them. And straightway their eyes were opened, and they [58] knew him; and he was taken away from them. And they said the one to the other, Was not our heart heavy within us, while he was speaking to us in the way, and interpreting to us the scriptures?

[59] And they rose in that hour, and returned to Jerusalem, and found the eleven [60] gathered, and those that were with them, saying, Truly our Lord is risen, and hath [61] appeared to Simon. And they related what happened in the way, and how they knew him when he brake the bread. Neither believed they that also.

Section LIV.

[1] And while they talked together, the evening of that day arrived which was the First-day; and the doors were shut where the disciples were, because of the fear of the [2] Jews; and Jesus came and stood among them, and said unto them, Peace *be* with you: I am he; fear not. But they were agitated, and became afraid, and supposed that they [3] saw a spirit. Jesus said unto them, Why are ye agitated? And why do thoughts rise [4] [Arabic, p. 205] in your hearts? See my hands and my feet, that I am he: feel me, and know that a spirit hath not flesh and bones, as ye see me having that. [5] And when he had said this, he shewed them his hands and his feet and his side. [6] And they were until this time unbelieving, from their joy and

their wonder. He [7] said unto them, Have ye anything here to eat? And they gave him a portion of broiled fish and of honey. And he took *it*, and ate before them.

[8] And he said unto them, These are the sayings which I spoke unto you, while I was with you, that everything must be fulfilled, which is written in the law of [9] Moses, and the prophets, and the psalms, concerning me. Then opened he their [10] heart, that they might understand the scriptures; and he said unto them, Thus it is written, and thus it is necessary that the Messiah suffer, and rise from among the [11] dead on the third day; and *that* repentance unto the forgiveness of sins be preached [12] in his name among all the peoples; and the beginning shall be from Jerusalem. And [13] ye shall be witnesses of that. And I send unto you the promise of my Father. And [14] when the disciples heard that, they were glad. And Jesus said unto them again, [15] Peace *be* with you: as my Father hath sent me, I also send you. And when he had said this, he breathed on them, and said unto them, Receive ye the Holy Spirit: [16] and if ye forgive sins to *any* man, they shall be forgiven him; and if ye retain them against *any* man, they shall be retained.

[17] But Thomas, one of the twelve, called Thama, was not there with the disciples [18] when Jesus came. The disciples therefore said unto him, We have seen our Lord. But he said unto them, If I do not see in his hands the places of the nails, and put on them my fingers, and pass my hand over his side, I will not believe.

[19] And after eight days, on the next First-day, the disciples were assembled again within, and Thomas with them. And Jesus came, the doors being shut, and stood [20] [Arabic, p. 206] in the midst, and said unto them, Peace *be* with you. And he said to Thomas, Bring

hither thy finger, and behold my hands; and bring *hither* [21] thy hand, and spread it on my side: and be not unbelieving, but believing. Thomas [22] answered and said unto him, My Lord and my God. Jesus said unto him, Now since thou hast seen me, thou hast believed: blessed are they that have not seen me, and have believed.

[23] And many other signs did Jesus before his disciples, and they are they which [24] are not written in this book: but these that are written also *are* that ye may believe in Jesus the Messiah, the Son of God; and *that* when ye have believed, ye may have in his name eternal life.

[25] And after that, Jesus shewed *himself* again to his disciples at the sea of Tiberias; [26] and he shewed *himself* unto them thus. And there were together Simon Cephas, and Thomas which was called Twin, and Nathanael who was of Cana of Galilee, [27] and the sons of Zebedee, and two other of the disciples. Simon Cephas said unto them, I go to catch fish. They said unto him, And we also come with thee. And they went forth, and went up into the boat; and in that night they caught nothing. [28] And when the morning arrived, Jesus stood on the shore of the sea: but the disciples [29] knew not that it was Jesus. And Jesus said unto them, Children, have ye anything [30] to eat? They said unto him, No. He said unto them, Cast your net from the right side of the boat, and ye shall find. And they threw, and they were not able [31] to draw the net for the abundance of the fish that were come into it. And that disciple whom Jesus loved said to Cephas, This is our Lord. And Simon, when he heard that it was our Lord, took his tunic, and girded it on his waist (for he was [32] naked), and cast himself into the sea to come to Jesus. But some others of the disciples

came in the boat (and they were not far from the land, but about two [33] [Arabic, p. 207] hundred cubits), and drew that net of fish. And when they went up on the [34] land, they saw live coals laid, and fish laid thereon, and bread. And Jesus [35] said unto them, Bring of this fish which ye have now caught. Simon Cephas therefore went up, and dragged the net to the land, full of great fish, a hundred and fifty-three [36] fishes: and with all this weight that net was not rent. And Jesus said unto them, Come and sit down. And no man of the disciples dared to ask him who he was, for they knew that it was our Lord. But he did not appear to them in his *own* [37, 38] form. And Jesus came, and took bread and fish, and gave unto them. This is the third time that Jesus appeared to his disciples, when he had risen from among the dead.

[39] And when they had breakfasted, Jesus said to Simon Cephas, Simon, son of Jonah, loves thou me more than these? He said unto him, Yea, my Lord; thou [40] knows that I love thee. Jesus said unto him, Feed for me my lambs. He said unto him again a second time, Simon, son of Jonah, loves thou me? He said unto him, Yea, my Lord; thou knows that I love thee. He said unto him, Feed for [41] me my sheep. He said unto him again the third time, Simon, son of Jonah, loves thou me? And it grieved Cephas that he said unto him three times, Loves thou me? He said unto him, My Lord, thou knows everything; thou knows that I [42] love thee. Jesus said unto him, Feed for me my sheep. Verily, verily, I say unto thee, When thou was a child, thou didst gird thy waist for thyself, and go whither [Arabic, p. 208] thou would: but when thou shalt be old, thou shalt stretch out thy hands, and another shall gird thy waist, and take thee whither thou would not. [43] He said that to him to explain by what death he was to

glorify God. And when he [44] had said that, he said unto him, Come after me. And Simon Cephas turned, and saw that disciple whom Jesus loved following him; he which at the supper leaned on [45] Jesus' breast, and said, My Lord, who is it that betrayed thee? When therefore Cephas saw him, he said to Jesus, My Lord, and this *man*, what shall be in his [46] case? Jesus said unto him, If I will that this *man* remain until I come, what is [47] that to thee? Follow thou me. And this word spread among the brethren, that that disciple should not die: but Jesus said not that he should not die; but, If I will that this *man* remain until I come, what is that to thee?

[48] This is the disciple which bare witness of that, and wrote it: and we know that his witness is true.

Section LV.

[1] But the eleven disciples went into Galilee, to the mountain where Jesus had [2] appointed them. And when they saw him, they worshipped him: but there were of [3] them who doubted. And while they sat there he appeared to them again, and upbraided *them* for their lack of faith and the hardness of their hearts, those that saw him when he was risen, and believed not.

[4] [Arabic, p. 209] Then said Jesus unto them, I have been given all authority in heaven [5] and earth; and as my Father hath sent me, so I also send you. Go now into [6] all the world, and preach my gospel in all the creation; and teach all the peoples, and [7] baptize them in the name of the Father and the Son and the Holy Spirit; and teach them to keep all whatsoever I commanded you: and lo, I am with you all the days, unto [8] the end of the world. For whosoever believeth and is baptized shall be saved; but [9] whosoever believeth not shall be rejected.

And the signs which shall attend those that believe in me are these: that they shall cast out devils in my name; and they [10] shall speak with new tongues; and they shall take *up* serpents, and if they drink deadly poison, it shall not injure them; and they shall lay their hands on the diseased, [11] and they shall be healed. But ye, abide in the city of Jerusalem, until ye be clothed with power from on high.

[12] And our Lord Jesus, after speaking to them, took them out to Bethany: and he [13] lifted up his hands, and blessed them. And while he blessed them, he was separated from them, and ascended into heaven, and sat down at the right hand of God. [14, 15] And they worshipped him, and returned to Jerusalem with great joy: and at all times they were in the temple, praising and blessing God. Amen.

[16] And from thence they went forth, and preached in every place; and our Lord helped them, and confirmed their sayings by the signs which they did.

[17] And here are also many other things which Jesus did, which if they were written every one of them, not even the world, according to my opinion, would contain the books which should be written.

Subscriptions.
I. In Borgian ms.
Here ended the Gospel which Tatianus compiled and named *Diatessaron*, i.e., The Fourfold, a compilation from the four Gospels of the holy Apostles, the excellent Evangelists (peace be upon them). It was translated by the excellent and learned priest, Abu'l Faraj 'Abdulla ibn-at-Tayyib (may God grant him favor), from Syriac into Arabic, from an exemplar written by 'Isa ibn-'Ali al-

Motatabbib, pupil of Honain ibn-Ishak (God have mercy on them both). Amen.

2. In Vatican ms.

Here ended, by the help of God, the holy Gospel that Titianus compiled from the four Gospels, which is known as *Diatessaron*. And praise be to God, as he is entitled to it and lord of it! And to him be the glory forever.

Find this and other great works of the Early Church Fathers at lighthousechristianpublishing.com.

Our Father who art in heaven, hallowed be thy name.
Thy kingdom come, Thy will be done, on earth as it is in heaven.
Give us this day our daily bread and forgive us our trespasses as we forgive those who trespass against us.
And lead us not into temptation, but deliver us from evil, for Thine is the kingdom, the power and the glory. Forever and ever.

Amen

Hail Mary full of grace, the Lord is with thee.
Blessed art thou amongst women and blessed is the fruit
of thy womb Jesus. Holy Mary mother of God, pray for us
sinners, now and the hour of our death.

www.ingramcontent.com/pod-product-compliance
Lightning Source LLC
Chambersburg PA
CBHW052137070526
44585CB00017B/1866